A-Z COLCH...

CW00430554

Key to Map Pages	2-3
Map Pages	4-41
Large Scale Town Centre	42

Index to...
Villages...
and sele...

REFERENCE

A Road	A134	Church or Chapel	†
B Road	B1137	Cycleway (selected)	
Dual Carriageway		Fire Station	■
One-way Street		Hospital	(H)
Traffic flow on A Roads is also indicated by a heavy line on the driver's left.		House Numbers (A & B Roads only)	189 · 38
Road Under Construction		Information Centre	🄸
Opening dates are correct at the time of publication.		National Grid Reference	600
Proposed Road		Park & Ride	Colchester P+R
Junction Name	CROWN INTERCHANGE	Police Station	▲
Restricted Access		Post Office	★
Pedestrianized Road		Safety Camera with Speed Limit	(30)
Track / Footpath		Fixed cameras and long term road works cameras. Symbols do not indicate camera direction.	
Residential Walkway			

Toilet:
without facilities for the Disabled	▽
with facilities for the Disabled	▽
Disabled use only	▽

Railway	Level Crossing / Station / Tunnel		
Built-up Area	QUEEN ST	Educational Establishment	
City Wall (large scale only)		Hospital or Healthcare Building	
Local Authority Boundary	–·–·–	Industrial Building	
Posttown Boundary		Leisure or Recreational Facility	
Postcode Boundary (within posttown)		Place of Interest	
Map Continuation	14 · Large Scale Town Centre 42	Public Building	
		Shopping Centre & Market	
Car Park (selected)	P	Other Selected Buildings	

SCALE

Map Pages 4-41   1:19000

0 ¼ ½ Mile
0 250 500 750 Metres
3.33 inches (8.47cm) to 1 mile   5.26cm to 1 kilometre

Map Page 42   1:9500

0 ⅛ ¼ Mile
0 100 200 300 Metres
6.67 inches (16.94cm) to 1 mile   10.53cm to 1 kilometre

EDITION 5 2015
Copyright © Geographers' A-Z Map Co. Ltd.
Telephone: 01732 781000 (Enquiries & Trade Sales)
01732 783422 (Retail Sales)
© Crown copyright and database rights 2015 OS 100017302.
Safety camera information supplied by www.PocketGPSWorld.com
Speed Camera Location Database Copyright 2015 © PocketGPSWorld.com

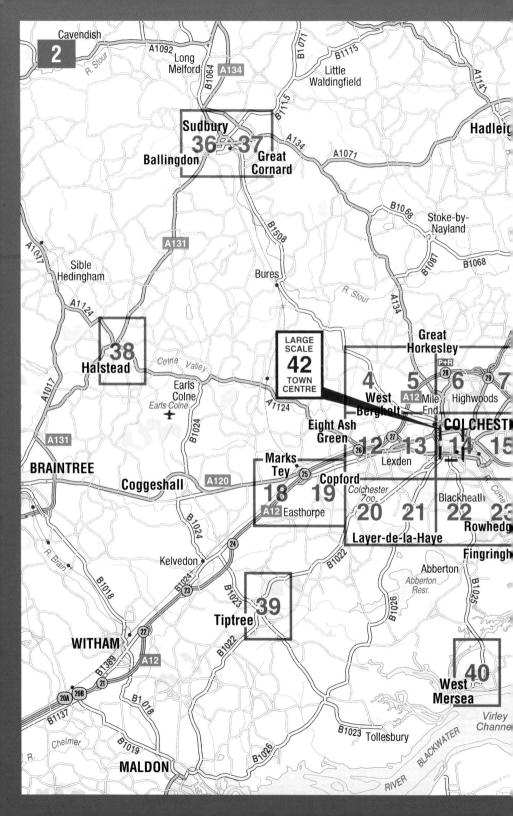

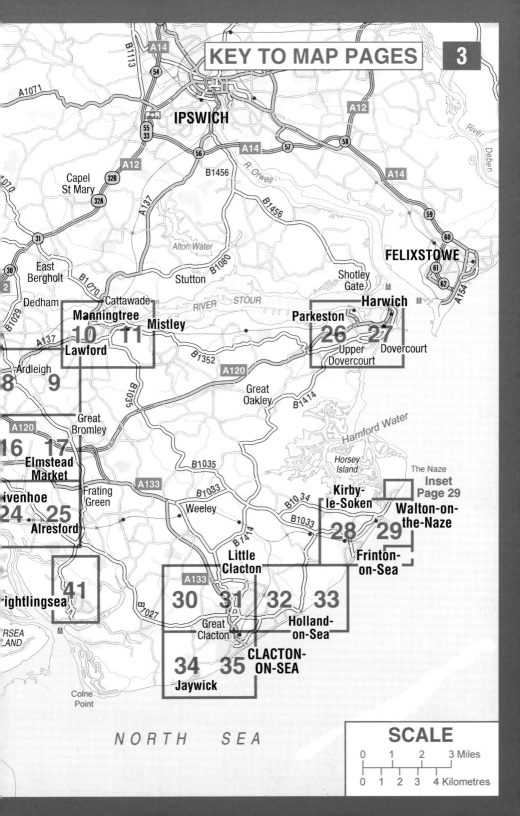

KEY TO MAP PAGES

NORTH SEA

SCALE

0   1   2   3 Miles

0 1 2 3   4 Kilometres

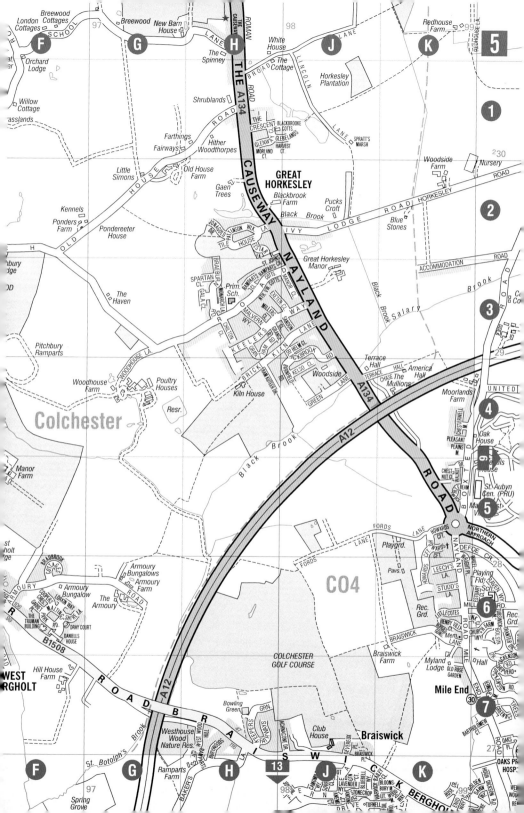

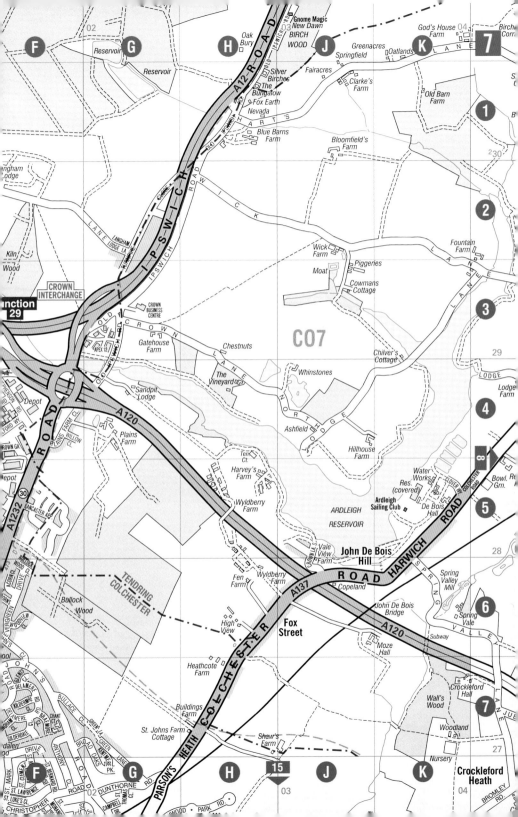

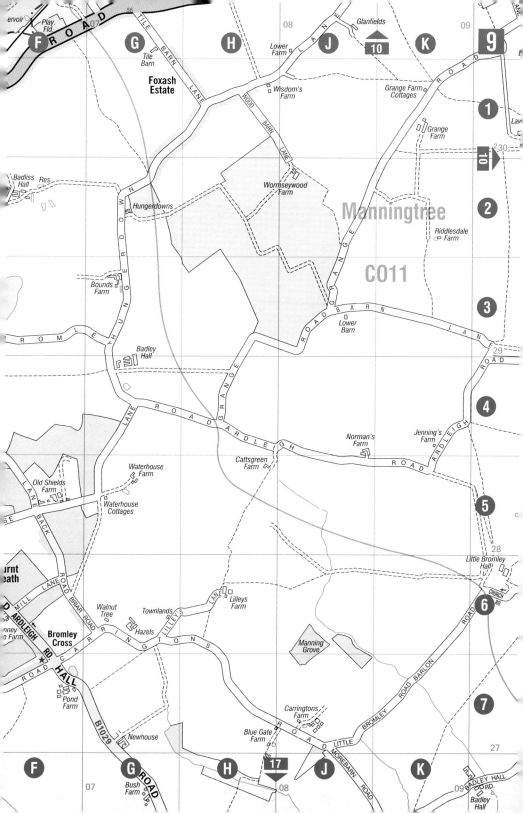

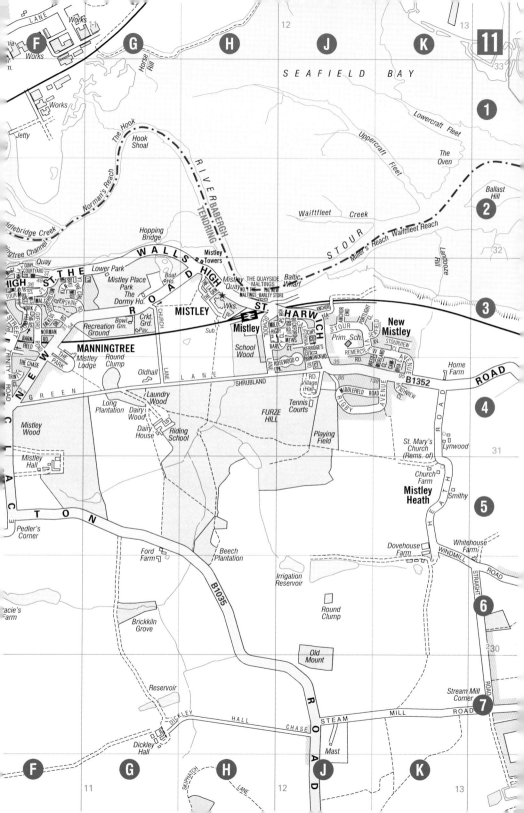

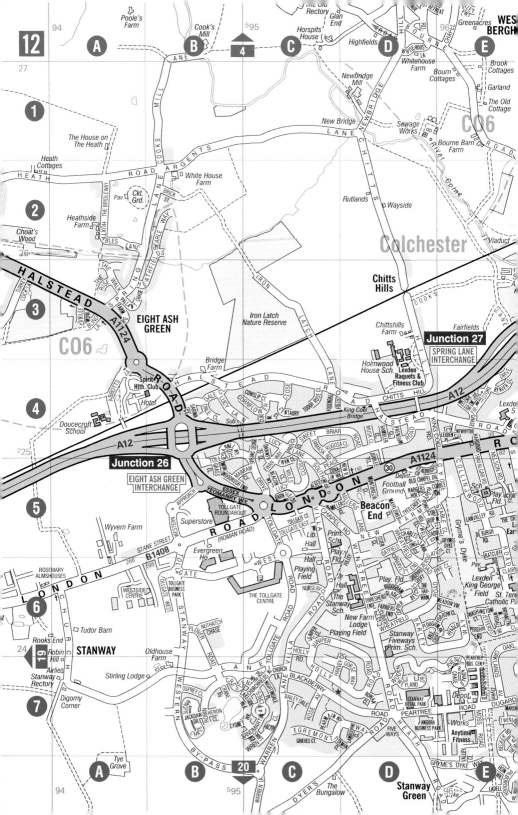

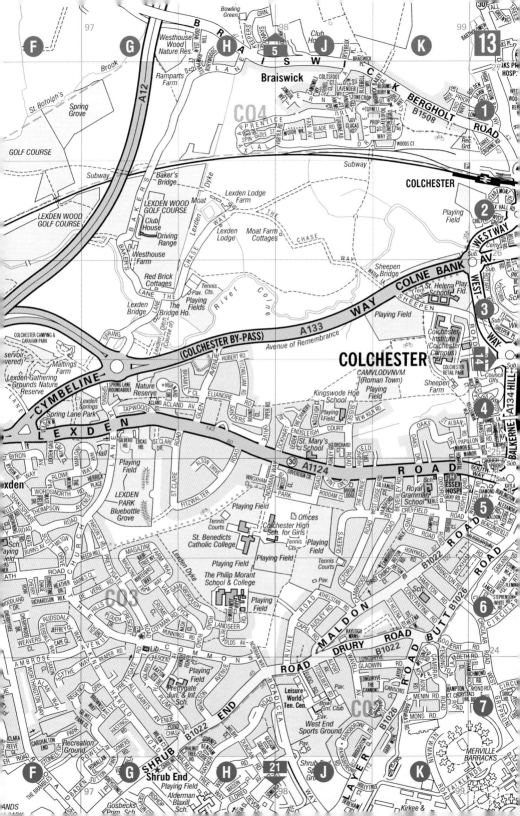

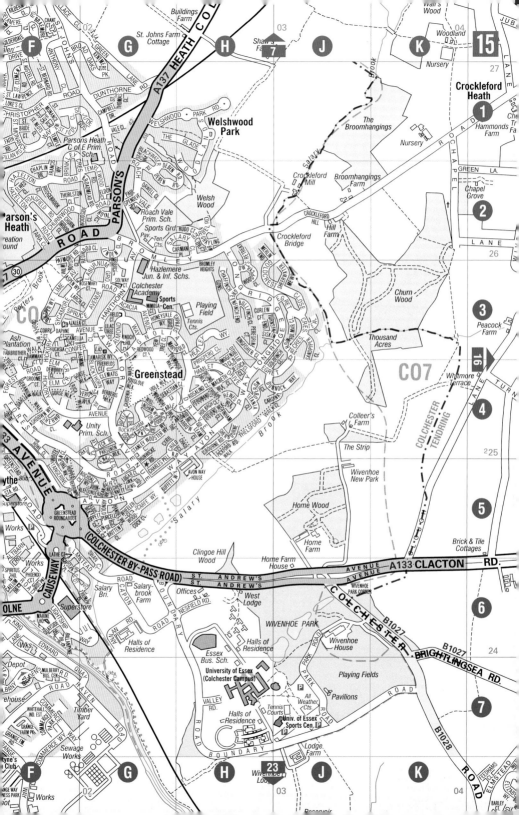

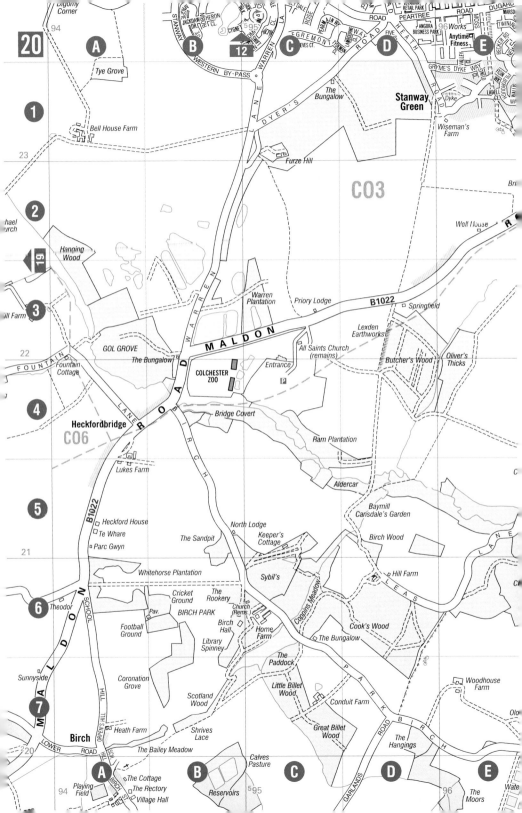

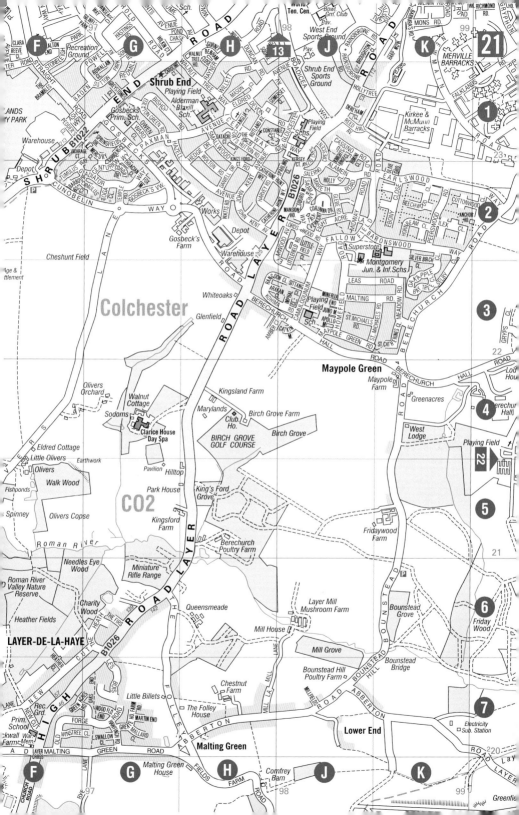

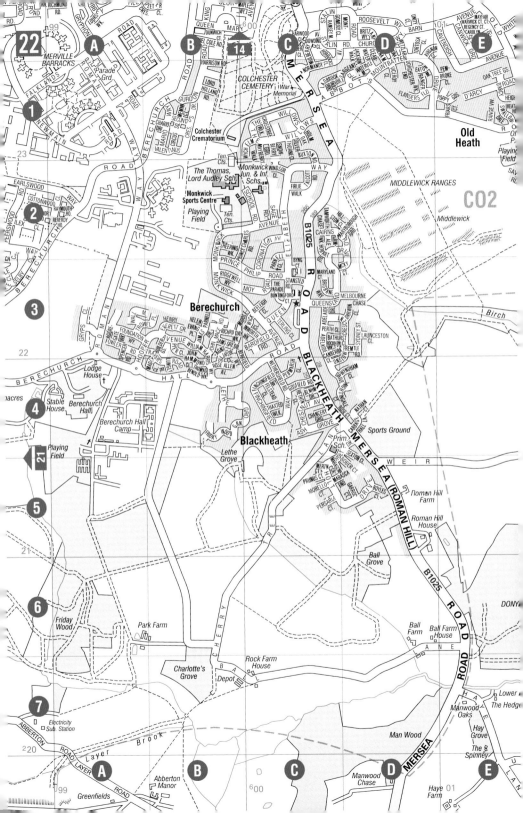

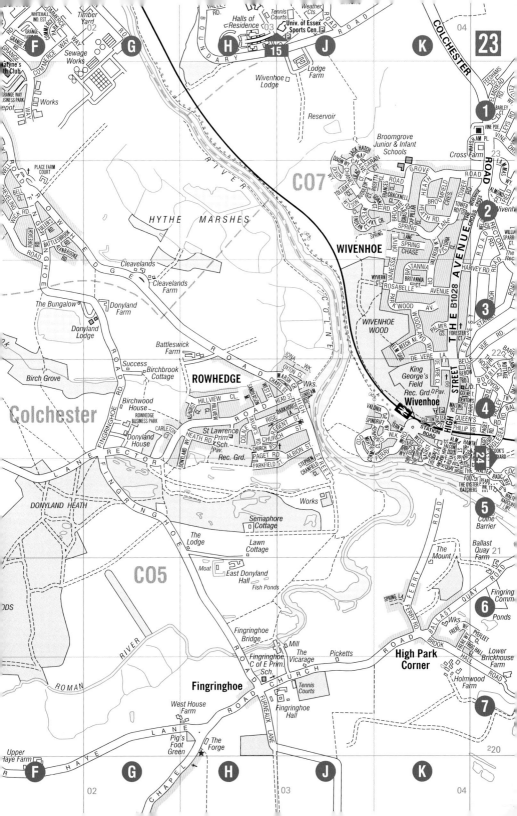

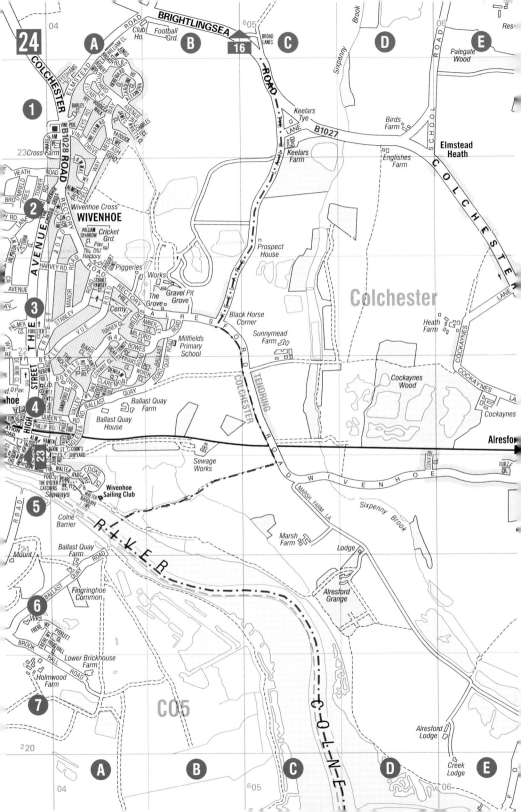

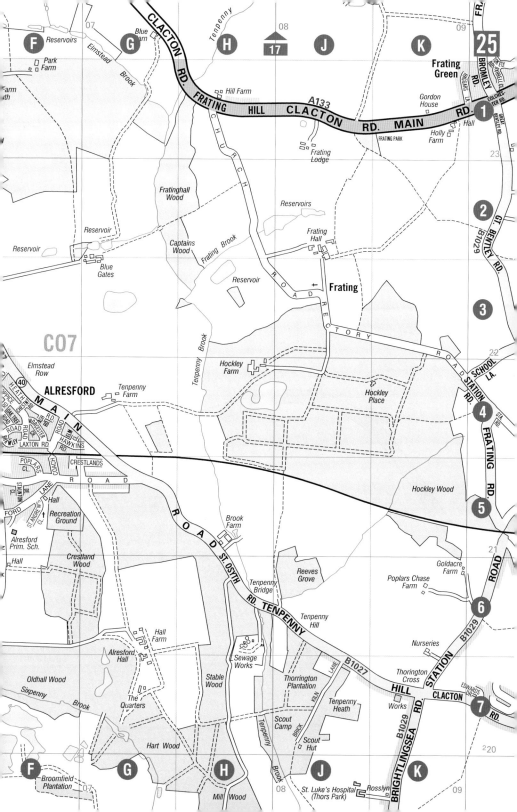

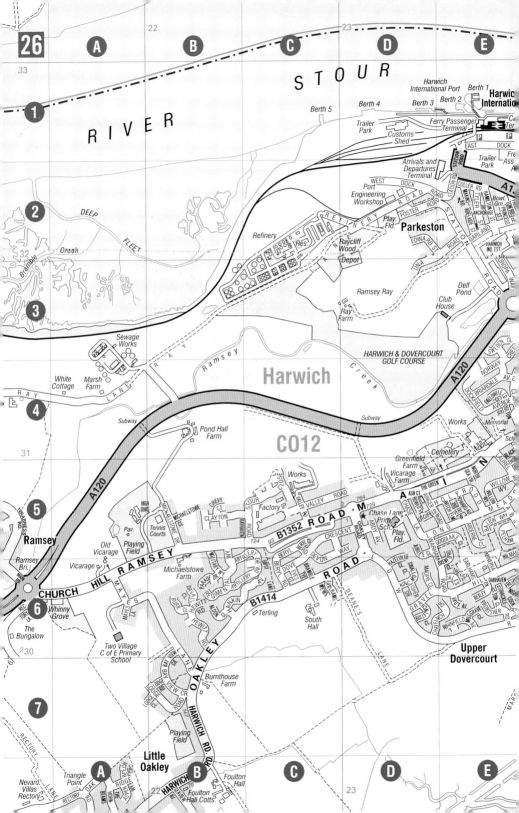

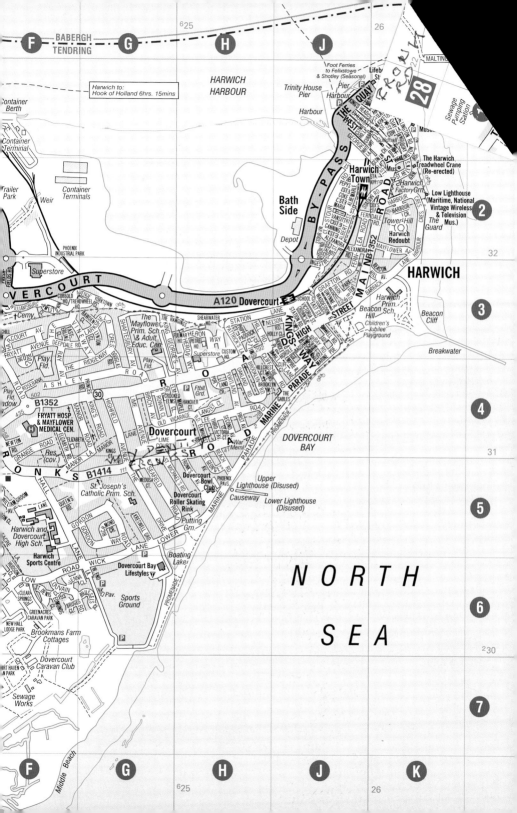

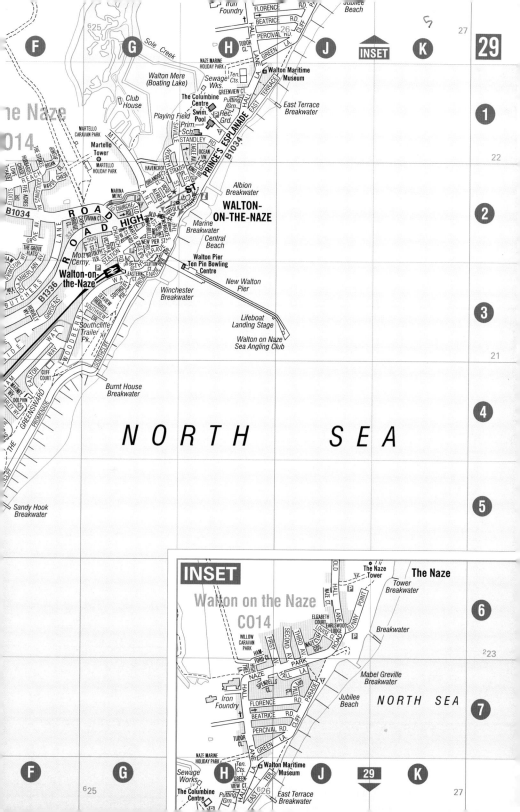

Map labels (main map)

625

Sole Creek

Iron Foundry

FLORENCE

BEATRICE RD.

PERCIVAL RD.

Jubilee Beach

27

INSET

Walton Mere (Boating Lake)

NAZE MARINE HOLIDAY PARK

Sewage Wks.

Walton Maritime Museum

Ten. Cts.

GREENVIEW CT.

EAST TERRACE

TUDOR CL.

GREEN LA.

LANE

The Naze

2014

Club House

The Columbine Centre

Putting Grn.

Rec. Grd.

Swim. Pool

Prim. Sch.

East Terrace Breakwater

1

Martello Caravan Park

Playing Field

STANDLEY

EAGLE AV.

22

Martello Tower

PRINCE'S ESPLANADE

B1034

OCEAN VW.

Martello Holiday Park

HAVENCROFT

CUMBERLAND

STRATFORD

KING'S

Albion Breakwater

WALTON-ON-THE-NAZE

2

Marina Mews

ROAD

HIGH

CHURCH

VIVIAN CT.

ST.

NEW PIER

SUFFOLK

PARADE

OLD PIER

Marine Breakwater

Central Beach

B1034

The Grove Flats

GROVE AV.

Mott Botolph's Cemy.

STATION

CLIFTON

EASTERN

TERRACE

Walton Pier

Ten Pin Bowling Centre

3

BUTCHERS

B1336

Walton-on-the-Naze

SEAVIEW

SOUTHVIEW

DR.

Southcliffe Trailer Pk.

Winchester Breakwater

New Walton Pier

Lifeboat Landing Stage

Walton on Naze Sea Angling Club

21

WOODBERRY

GREENSWARD

PROMENADE

DOLPHIN

CLIFF COURT

Burnt House Breakwater

4

NORTH   SEA

Sandy Hook Breakwater

5

INSET

INSET

Walton on the Naze

CO14

OLD HALL LANE

The Naze Tower

The Naze

Tower Breakwater

Breakwater

6

WILLOW CARAVAN PARK

FIRST AV.

SECOND AV.

THIRD AV.

PARK

Elizabeth Court

Earlswood

WATER CT.

LOUISE CT.

SONNY POINT

EDS.

Mabel Greville Breakwater

23

HAM. FORD CL.

ALL LA.

SPENDELLS CL.

CLIFF PARADE

Jubilee Beach

NORTH SEA

7

Iron Foundry

FLORENCE

BEATRICE RD.

PERCIVAL RD.

TUDOR LA.

GREEN LA.

EAST TER.

HALL

NAZE MARINE HOLIDAY PARK

Ten. Cts.

GREENVIEW CT.

Sewage Works

The Columbine Centre

Putting Grn.

Walton Maritime Museum

East Terrace Breakwater

625

626

27

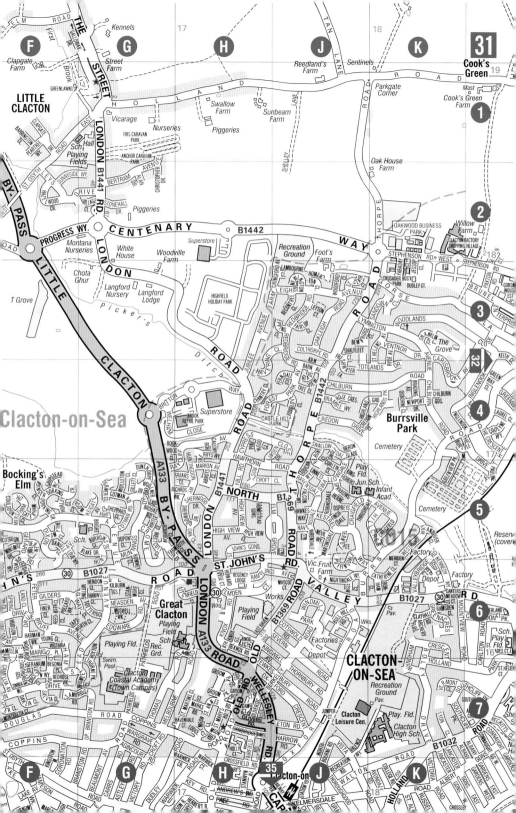

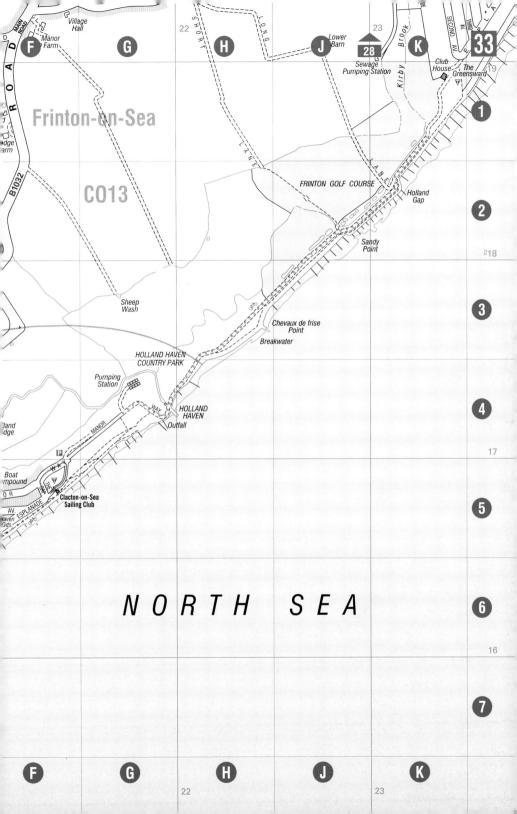

Village
Hall

Manor
Farm

F

G

H

J

Lower
Barn

23

28

Sewage
Pumping Station

Club
House

K

The
Greensward

33

19

Frinton-on-Sea

CO13

SHORT

22

LONG

Kirby Brook

MAIN ROAD

SECOND AV.

THIRD

LA

1

FRINTON GOLF COURSE

Holland
Gap

2

²18

Sandy
Point

LANE

B1032

ROAD

dge
arm

Sheep
Wash

Chevaux de frise
Point

3

Breakwater

HOLLAND HAVEN
COUNTRY PARK

Pumping
Station

4

land
dge

WAY

HOLLAND
HAVEN

17

MANOR

Outfall

P

Boat
mpound

WAY

NOR

5

ESPLANADE

AV.

Clacton-on-Sea
Sailing Club

aven
ds

ROAD

N O R T H   S E A

6

16

7

F

G

H

J

K

22

23

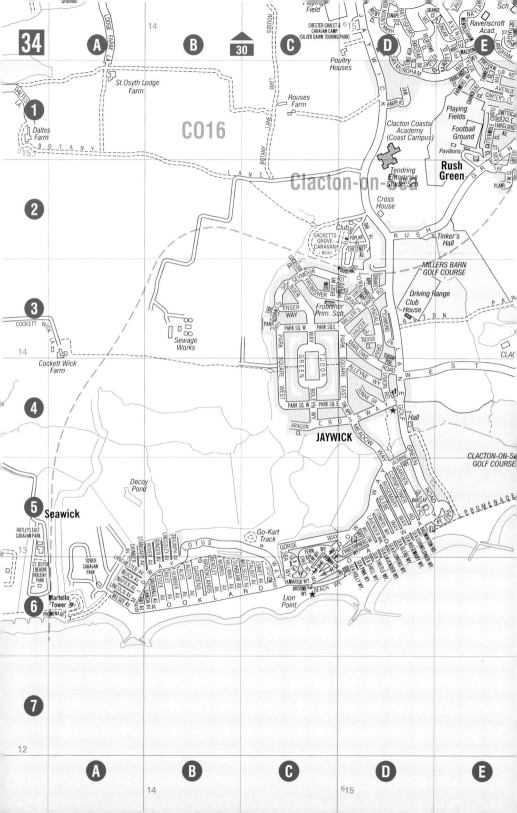

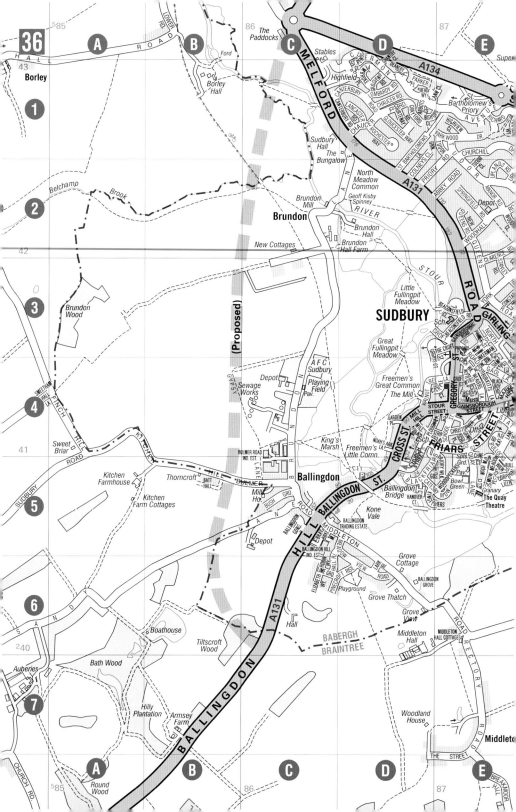

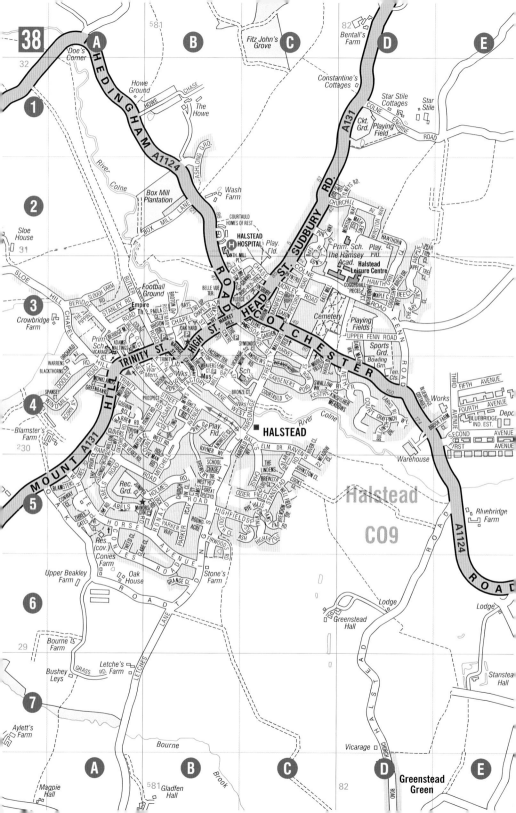

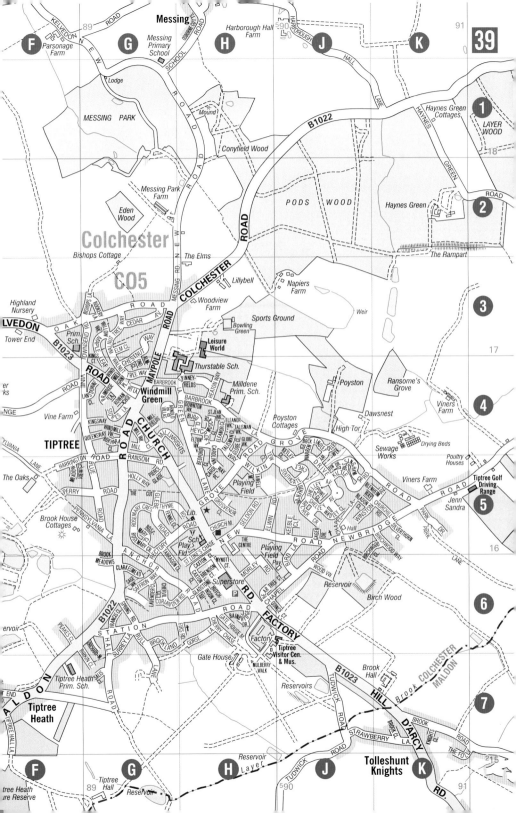

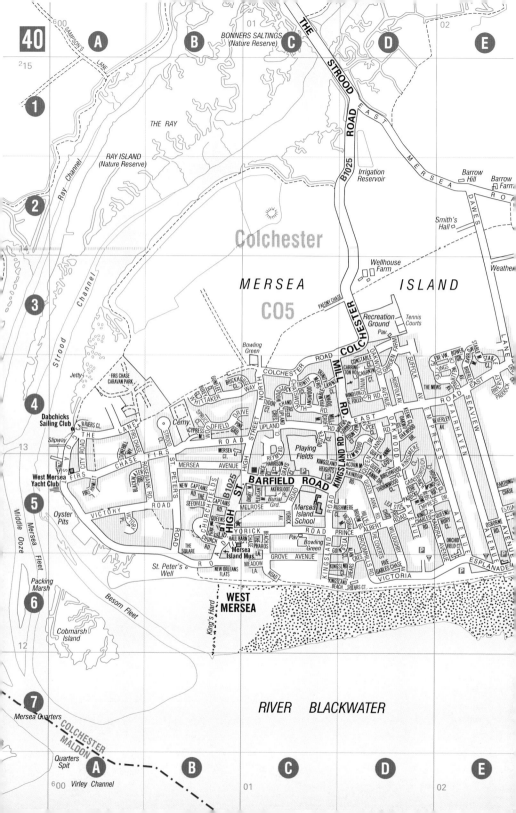

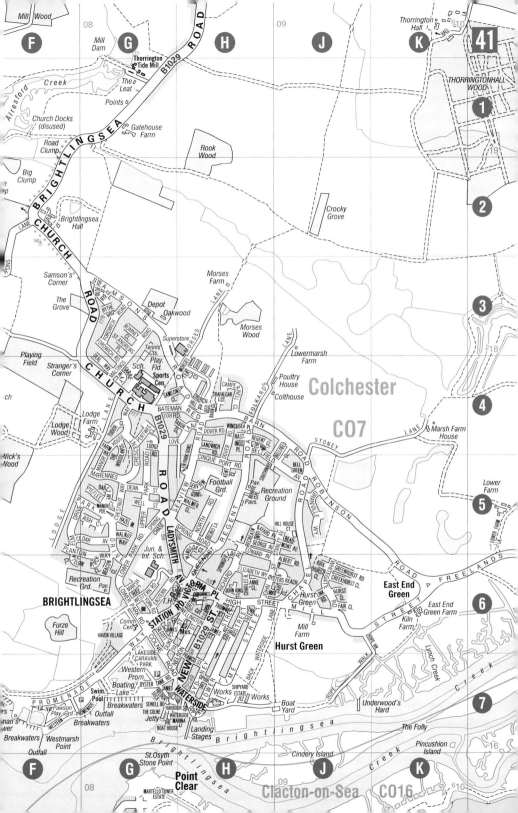

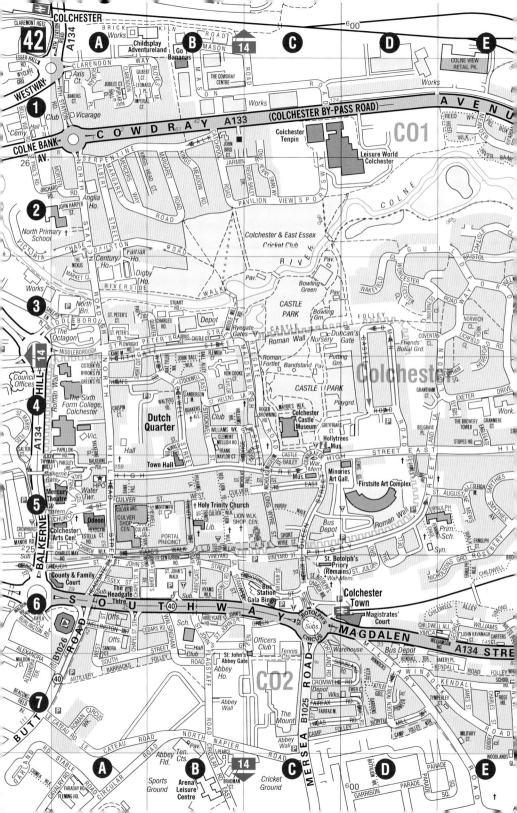

INDEX

Including Streets, Places & Areas, Hospitals etc., Industrial Estates,
Selected Flats & Walkways, Junction Names, Stations and Selected Places of Interest.

HOW TO USE THIS INDEX

1. Each street name is followed by its Postcode District, then by its Locality abbreviation(s) and then by its map reference;
e.g. **Abberton Rd.** CO2: Lay H . . . .7H **21** is in the CO2 Postcode District and the Layer-de-la-Haye Locality and is to be found in square 7H on page **21**.
The page number is shown in bold type.

2. A strict alphabetical order is followed in which Av., Rd., St., etc. (though abbreviated) are read in full and as part of the street name;
e.g. **Brook Lodge** appears after **Brooklands Gdns.** but before **Brooklyn Ct.**

3. Streets and a selection of flats and walkways that cannot be shown on the mapping, appear in the index with the thoroughfare to which they are
connected shown in brackets; e.g. **Albemarle Ho.** CO12: Har . . . .2J **27** (off Albemarle St.)

4. Addresses that are in more than one part are referred to as not continuous.

5. Places and areas are shown in the index in BLUE TYPE and the map reference is to the actual map square in which the town centre or area is located
and not to the place name shown on the map; e.g. BEACON END. . . .5C **12**

6. An example of a selected place of interest is **Boxted Airfield Mus.** 1E **6**

7. Examples of stations are:
Alresford Station (Rail) . . . .4E **24**; **Colchester Bus Station** . . . .6C **42**; **Colchester (Park & Ride)** 3A **6**

8. Junction names are shown in the index in BOLD CAPITAL TYPE; e.g. **CROWN INTERCHANGE** 3G **7**

9. An example of a Hospital, Hospice or selected Healthcare Faciity is **CLACTON & DISTRICT HOSPITAL** 3H **35**

10. Map references for entries that appear on large scale page **42** are shown first, with small scale map references shown in brackets;
e.g. **Abbeygate St.** CO2: Colc 6B **42** (5B **14**)

GENERAL ABBREVIATIONS

All. : Alley	**Fld.** : Field	**Pk.** : Parky
App. : Approach	**Flds.** : Fields	**Pas.** : Passage
Arc. : Arcade	**Gdn.** : Garden	**Pl.** : Place
Av. : Avenue	**Gdns.** : Gardens	**Pct.** : Precinct
Bk. : Back	**Ga.** : Gate	**Prom.** : Promenade
Blvd. : Boulevard	**Gt.** : Great	**Ri.** : Rise
Bri. : Bridge	**Grn.** : Green	**Rd.** : Road
Bldg. : Building	**Gro.** : Grove	**Rdbt.** : Roundabout
Bldgs. : Buildings	**Hgts.** : Heights	**Shop.** : Shopping
Bus. : Business	**Ho.** : House	**Sth.** : South
Cvn. : Caravan	**Ind.** : Industrial	**Sq.** : Square
C'way. : Causeway	**Info.** : Information	**Sta.** : Station
Cen. : Centre	**La.** : Lane	**St.** : Street
Chu. : Church	**Lit.** : Little	**Ter.** : Terrace
Cir. : Circus	**Lwr.** : Lower	**Twr.** : Tower
Cl. : Close	**Mans.** : Mansions	**Trad.** : Trading
Comn. : Common	**Mdw.** : Meadow	**Up.** : Upper
Cnr. : Corner	**Mdws.** : Meadows	**Va.** : Vale
Cotts. : Cottages	**M.** : Mews	**Vw.** : View
Ct. : Court	**Mt.** : Mount	**Vs.** : Villas
Cres. : Crescent	**Mus.** : Museum	**Vis.** : Visitors
Cft. : Croft	**Nth.** : North	**Wlk.** : Walk
Dr. : Drive	**No.** : Number	**W.** : West
E. : East	**Pde.** : Parade	**Yd.** : Yard
Est. : Estate		

LOCALITY ABBREVIATIONS

Abberton: CO5 . . . . .Abb	**Frinton-on-Sea:** CO13-14 . . . . .Frin S	**Little Cornard:** CO10 . . . . .L Cor
Aldham: CO6 . . . . .Aldh	**Great Bentley:** CO7,CO16 . . . . .Gt Ben	**Little Horkesley:** CO6 . . . . .L Hork
Alresford: CO7 . . . . .Alr	**Great Bromley:** CO7,CO11 . . . . .Gt Bro	**Little Oakley:** CO12 . . . . .L Oak
Ardleigh: CO4,CO7,CO11 . . . . .A'lgh	**Great Cornard:** CO10 . . . . .Gt Cor	**Little Tey:** CO6 . . . . .L Tey
Ballingdon: CO10 . . . . .Ball	**Great Holland:** CO13 . . . . .Gt Hol	**Manningtree:** CO11 . . . . .Mann
Birch: CO2 . . . . .B'ch	**Great Horkesley:** CO6 . . . . .Gt Hork	**Marks Tey:** CO6 . . . . .M Tey
Borley: CO10 . . . . .Borl	**Great Oakley:** CO12 . . . . .Gt Oak	**Messing:** CO5 . . . . .Mess
Boxted: CO4,CO6 . . . . .Boxt	**Great Tey:** CO6 .Gt Tey	**Middleton:** CO10 . . . . .Midd
Bradfield: CO11 . . . . .Brad	**Great Waldingfield:** CO10 . . . . .Gt Wal	**Mistley:** CO11 . . . . .Mist
Brantham: CO11 . . . . .Brant	**Greenstead Green:** CO9 . . . . .G'std G	**Peldon:** CO5 . . . . .Pel
Brightlingsea: CO7 . . . . .B'sea	**Halstead:** CO9 . . . . .Hals	**Point Clear:** CO16 . . . . .P'nt C
Bulmer: CO10 . . . . .Bulm	**Harwich:** CO12 . . . . .Har	**Ramsey:** CO12 . . . . .R'sy
Cattawade: CO11 . . . . .Catt	**Heckfordbridge:** CO2-3,CO6 . . . . .Heck	**Rowhedge:** CO5 . . . . .Rhdge
Clacton-on-Sea: CO13,CO15-16 . . . . .Clac S	**Holland-on-Sea:** CO15 . . . . .Hol S	**St Osyth:** CO16 .St O
Coggeshall: CO6 . . . . .Cogg	**Horsley Cross:** CO11 . . . . .Hor X	**Stanway:** CO3 . . . . .S'way
Colchester: CO1-4,CO7 . . . . .Colc	**Inworth:** CO5 . . . . .Inw	**Sudbury:** CO10 .Sud
Copford: CO6 . . . . .Cop	**Jaywick:** CO15 . . . . .Jay	**Thorrington:** CO7 . . . . .Thorr
Crockleford Heath: CO7 . . . . .Crock H	**Kirby Cross:** CO13 . . . . .Kir C	**Tiptree:** CO5 . . . . .Tip
Dedham: CO7 . . . . .Ded	**Kirby-le-Soken:** CO13 . . . . .Kir S	**Tolleshunt Knights:** CO5 . . . . .Tol K
Easthorpe: CO5 . . . . .Ethpe	**Langham:** CO4,CO7 . . . . .L'ham	**Walton-on-the-Naze:** CO13-14 . . . . . . .Walt
Eight Ash Green: CO6 . . . . .Eig G	**Lawford:** CO7,CO11 . . . . .Law	**Weeley:** CO16 . . . . .Wee
Elmstead Market: CO7 . . . . .Elm M	**Layer Breton:** CO2 . . . . .Lay B	**Weeley Heath:** CO16 . . . . .Wee H
Feering: CO5 . . . . .Fee	**Layer-de-la-Haye:** CO2 . . . . .Lay H	**West Bergholt:** CO6 . . . . .W Ber
Fingringhoe: CO5 . . . . .Fing	**Layer Marney:** CO5 . . . . .Lay M	**West Mersea:** CO5 . . . . .W Mer
Fordham: CO6 . . . . .For	**Little Bentley:** CO7 . . . . .L Ben	**Wivenhoe:** CO7 . . . . .W'hoe
Fordham Heath: CO3 . . . . .Ford H	**Little Bromley:** CO7,CO11 . . . . .L Bro	**Wormingford:** CO6 . . . . .Wmgfd
Frating: CO7 . . . . .Frat	**Little Clacton:** CO16 . . . . .L Cla	**Wrabness:** CO12 . . . . .Wrab

A

Abbas Wlk. CO10: Gt Cor 6J 37
ABBERTON DAY HOSPITAL 7B 6
(within Colchester General Hospital)
Abberton Rd. CO2: Lay H 7H 21
Abbey Ct. CO2: Colc 6C 14
ABBEY FIELD 7A 14
Abbey Fld. Vw. CO2: Colc 7A 14
Abbeygate Ho. CO2: Colc 6B 42
Abbeygate St. CO2: Colc 6B 42 (5B 14)
Abbey Rd. CO10: Sud 2E 36
Abbigail Gdns. CO15: Clac S 7A 32
Abbots Cl. CO15: Sud 1D 36
   CO15: Clac S 5H 31
Abbot's Rd. CO2: Colc 1C 22
Abbott Rd. CO12: Har 5E 26
Abbotts La. CO6: Eig G 4A 12
Abdy Av. CO12: Har 5D 26
Abels Rd. CO9: Hals 5A 38
Acacia Av. CO4: Colc 3G 15
Accommodation Rd.
   CO4: Boxt 3K 5
Achnacone Dr. CO4: Colc 7J 5
Acland Av. CO10: Colc 4G 13
Acland Cl. CO3: Colc 4G 13
Acorn Av. CO9: Hals 4A 38
Acorn Cl. CO4: Colc 6F 7
   CO12: Har 6F 27
Acorn M. CO5: W Mer 5D 40
Acorn Pl. CO4: Colc 4E 6
Acorns, The CO15: Jay 3C 34
Acton Cl. CO10: Sud 3F 37
Acton La. CO10: Sud 1G 37
   (Hawkins Rd.)
   CO10: Sud 3F 37
   (Waldingfield Rd.)
Acton Sq. CO10: Sud 4E 36
Adams Ct. CO9: Hals 3A 38
Adams Maltings CO9: Hals 3A 38
Addison Rd. CO2: Colc 2G 37
Addis Rd. CO16: Clac S 5E 30
Adelaide Dr. CO2: Colc 3C 22
Adelaide St. CO12: Har 2E 26
Admirals Wlk. CO7: W'hoe 4K 23
Aerofoil Gro. CO4: Colc 1K 13
Affleck Rd. CO4: Colc 4G 15
Agar Rd. CO14: Walt 2G 29
Agate Rd. CO15: Clac S 2H 35
Aggregate Wlk. CO2: Colc 3A 22
Agincourt Rd. CO15: Clac S 7G 31
Agnes Silverside Cl.
   CO2: Colc 3B 22
Ainger Rd. CO12: Har 5D 26
Aisne Rd. CO2: Colc 7K 13
Akersloot Pl. CO5: W Mer 5C 40
Alamein Rd. CO2: Colc 2J 21
Alanbrooke Rd. CO2: Colc 2F 23
Alan Dr. CO16: L Cla 2G 31
Alan Way CO3: Colc 7F 13
Albany Chase CO15: Clac S 7A 32
Albany Cl. CO6: W Ber 6E 4
Albany Gdns. CO2: Colc 7F 15
Albany Gdns. E. CO15: Clac S 7A 32
Albany Gdns. W. CO15: Clac S 7K 31
Albany Rd. CO6: W Ber 6E 4
Albemarle Ho. *CO12: Har* 2J 27
   (off Albemarle St.)
Albemarle St. CO12: Har 2J 27
Albert Gdns. CO15: Clac S 1K 35
Albertine Cl. CO3: S'way 5C 12
Albert Rd. CO7: B'sea 6J 41
Albert St. CO1: Colc 2A 42 (3A 14)
   CO12: Har 2J 27
Albion Gro. CO2: Colc 6C 14
Albion St. CO5: Rhdge 4J 23
Albrighton Cft. CO4: Colc 6E 6
Aldeburgh Cl. CO16: Clac S 7E 30
Aldeburgh Gdns. CO4: Colc 6D 6
Aldercar Rd. CO6: Cop 4J 19
Alderman Howe Lodge
   CO4: Colc 6D 6
   (off Tynedale Sq.)
Alderton Rd. CO4: Colc 3E 14
Alder Way CO10: Sud 3F 37
Aldon Cl. CO12: Har 6B 26
Alec Kay Ct. *CO2: Colc* 2J 21
   (off Layer Rd.)
Alefounder Cl. CO4: Colc 5G 15
Alexandra Av. CO5: W Mer 5D 40
Alexandra Dr. CO7: W'hoe 1A 24
Alexandra Ho. *CO12: Har* 4J 27
   (off Marine Pde.)

Alexandra Rd. CO3: Colc 6A 42 (5A 14)
   CO10: Sud 4G 37
   (Newton Rd.)
   CO10: Sud 3G 37
   (Windham Rd.)
   CO12: Har 2J 27
   CO15: Clac S 1H 35
Alexandra St. CO12: Har 2J 27
Alexandra Ter. CO3: Colc 7A 42 (5A 14)
Alfells Rd. CO7: Elm M 6D 16
Alfred Ter. CO14: Walt 2G 29
Alice Twyman Ho. CO1: Colc 5A 42
Allendale Dr. CO6: Cop 2H 19
Alleyne Way CO15: Jay 4D 34
Allfields CO12: Har 5E 26
All Saints Av. CO3: Colc 7G 13
Alma Sq. *CO11: Mann* 3F 11
   (off High St.)
Alma St. CO7: W'hoe 4K 23
Almond Cl. CO5: Tip 4G 39
   CO7: W'hoe 2A 24
   CO15: Clac S 1F 35
Almond Way CO4: Colc 3G 15
Alport Av. CO2: Colc 7J 13
ALRESFORD 4F 25
Alresford Rd. CO7: Alr, W'hoe 3B 24
Alresford Station (Rail) 4E 24
Altbarn Cl. *CO4: Colc* 5E 6
Altbarn Rd. CO2: Colc 5F 15
Alton Dr. CO3: Colc 5H 13
Alton Pk. Rd. CO15: Clac S 2G 35
   (Link Rd.)
   CO15: Clac S 3D 34
   (Richmond Dr.)
Alton Rd. CO15: Clac S 2H 35
Alverton Way CO4: Colc 7D 6
Alvis Av. CO15: Jay 6B 34
Alyssum Wlk. CO4: Colc 4F 15
Amber Ct. CO2: Colc 3H 21
Amberley Cl. CO7: W'hoe 3B 24
Ambleside Cl. CO15: Clac S 1K 35
Ambrose Av. CO3: Colc, S'way 7F 13
Ambrose Ct. CO6: Cop 2H 19
Amies Ct. CO2: Colc 6C 14
Anchorage, The CO12: Har 2E 26
Anchor End CO11: Mist 3J 11
Anchor Hill CO7: W'hoe 5K 23
Anchor Ho. CO2: Colc 2K 21
Anchor La. CO11: Mist 3J 11
Anchor Rd. CO5: Tip 5G 39
   CO15: Clac S 1G 35
Andover Cl. CO15: Clac S 5K 31
Anemone Ct. CO4: Colc 1J 13
Angel Ga. CO12: Har 1K 27
Anglefield CO15: Clac S 2J 35
Anglesea Rd. CO7: W'hoe 4A 24
Anglia Cl. CO2: Colc 1H 21
Angora Bus. Pk. CO3: S'way 7D 12
Annan Rd. CO4: Colc 6G 15
Anne Cl. CO7: B'sea 6H 41
Anson Cl. CO12: Har 5F 27
Anthony Cl. CO4: Colc 7F 7
Antonio Wlk. CO4: Colc 4H 15
Antonius Way CO4: Colc 4D 6
Anytime Fitness
   Colchester 7E 12
Anzio Cres. CO2: Colc 2J 21
Apex 12 CO7: A'lgh 3G 7
Apollo M. CO7: Colc 3J 21
Applegate M. CO10: Gt Cor 4H 37
Appleton M. CO4: Colc 4D 6
Apple Tree Cl. CO9: Hals 3D 38
Apprentice Dr. CO4: Colc 1H 13
Approach, The CO15: Jay 4D 34
Aquiline Ho. CO15: Clac S 4G 35
Aragon Cl. CO15: Jay 4C 34
Arakan Cl. CO2: Colc 3H 21
Arbour Way CO4: Colc 6E 6
Archer Cres. CO5: Tip 5J 39
Archery Flds. CO15: Clac S 6K 31
Arden Cl. CO4: Colc 7E 6
Arderne Cl. CO12: Har 5E 26
ARDLEIGH 3C 8
Ardleigh Ct. CO7: A'lgh 2C 8
ARDLEIGH HEATH 1B 8
Ardleigh Rd. CO7: Gt Bro 6F 9
   CO11: L Bro 4H 9
Ardleigh Sailing Club 5K 7
Arena Leisure Cen. 7B 42 (6B 14)
Argents La. CO3: Colc, Ford H 2B 12
Ariel Cl. CO4: Colc 4G 15
Armidale Wlk. CO2: Colc 2C 22
Armoury Rd. CO6: W Ber 6F 5
Arnold Dr. CO4: Colc 5G 15

Arnold Rd. CO15: Clac S 2G 35
Arnold Vs. CO5: Tip 4G 39
Arnstones Cl. CO4: Colc 3E 14
Arrow Rd. CO4: Colc 4H 15
Arrowsmith Wlk. CO4: Colc 4C 6
Arthur St. CO2: Colc 6C 42 (5B 14)
Artillery Barracks Folley
   CO2: Colc 7A 42 (5A 14)
Artillery Dr. CO12: Har 6B 26
Artillery St. CO1: Colc 5D 14
Asbury Cl. CO4: Colc 3F 15
Ascot M. CO15: Hol S 6B 32
Ashbury Dr. CO6: M Tey 3D 18
Ash Cl. CO7: B'sea 5G 41
   CO15: Clac S 1F 35
Ash Ct. CO12: Har 5D 26
Ashdown Way CO4: Colc 4F 15
Ashes Cl. CO14: Walt 2D 28
Ash Gro. CO2: Colc 4C 22
   CO7: W'hoe 1A 24
   CO10: Gt Cor 6J 37
Ashley Gdns. CO3: Colc 5J 13
Ashley Rd. CO12: Har 4F 27
Ashlong Gro. CO9: Hals 2B 38
Ashlyn's Rd. CO13: Frin S 6C 28
Ashmere Ri. CO10: Sud 3G 37
Ashmole Dr. CO13: Kir C 4D 28
Ash Ri. CO9: Hals 5C 38
Ash Rd. CO7: Alr 4F 25
Ashtead Cl. CO16: Clac S 5E 30
Ashurst Cl. CO5: Rhdge 4H 23
Ash Way CO3: Colc 1F 21
Ashwin Av. CO6: Cop 2H 19
Aspen Way CO4: Colc 3F 15
   CO12: L Oak 7A 26
Asquith Dr. CO4: Colc 5E 6
Astell Cl. CO13: Frin S 6D 28
Aster Cl. CO16: Clac S 7F 31
Astley Rd. CO15: Clac S 1G 35
Athelstan Rd. CO3: Colc 6J 13
Attlee Gdns. CO1: Colc 7D 42 (5C 14)
Attwood Cl. CO4: Colc 5D 6
Aubrey Dr. CO10: Sud 1G 37
Audley Rd. CO3: Colc 6J 13
Audley Way CO13: Frin S 4E 28
Audries Est. CO14: Walt 2E 28
Augustus Cl. CO4: Colc 4D 6
Austin Av. CO15: Jay 6B 34
Autoway CO4: Colc 5E 6
Autumn Cl. CO4: Colc 6F 31
Aveline Rd. CO7: A'lgh 3C 8
Avenue, The CO3: Colc 5J 13
   CO6: W Ber 7D 4
   CO7: W'hoe 3K 23
   CO15: Clac S 4A 32
Avignon Cl. CO2: Colc 7D 14
Avitus Way CO4: Colc 5D 6
Avocet Cl. CO5: W Mer 4E 40
   CO13: Kir C 4C 28
Avondale Rd. CO15: Clac S 1K 35
Avon Way *CO4: Colc* 5G 15
Avon Way Ho. CO4: Colc 5H 15
Axial Dr. CO4: Colc 1H 13
Axial Way CO4: Colc 4B 6
Aylesbury Dr. CO15: Hol S 5E 32
Ayloffe Rd. CO4: Colc 2E 14
Azalea Ct. CO4: Colc 3F 15
Azalea Way CO16: Clac S 7E 30

B

Back La. CO3: Colc 4E 12
Back La. E. CO7: Gt Bro 4K 17
Back La. W. CO7: Gt Bro 4K 17
Back Rd. CO7: A'lgh, Gt Bro 5F 9
Bk. Waterside La. CO7: B'sea 7H 41
Baden Powell Dr. CO3: Colc, S'way 1F 21
Badgers Grn. CO6: M Tey 3C 18
Badgers Holt CO3: S'way 5D 12
Badley Hall Rd. CO7: Gt Bro 2J 17
Badliss Hall La. CO7: A'lgh 2E 8
Badminton Rd. CO15: Jay 5D 34
Bagshaw Rd. CO12: Har 3J 27
Bailey Dale CO3: S'way 7C 12
Bainbridge Dr. CO5: Tip 6H 39
Baines Cl. CO3: Colc 6F 13
Bakers Cl. CO1: Colc 1A 42 (2A 14)
   CO10: Gt Cor 7G 37
Baker's La. CO3: Colc 2G 13
   CO4: Colc 2G 13
Bakery Pl. CO1: Colc 7E 42
Bale Cl. CO3: Colc 7E 12
Balfe Ct. CO4: Colc 5G 15
Balkerne Cl. CO1: Colc 4A 42 (4A 14)

Balkerne Gdns. CO1: Colc 5A 42 (4A 14)
Balkerne Hill CO3: Colc 5A 42 (4A 14)
Balkerne Pas. CO1: Colc 5A 42 (4A 14)
Ball All. CO1: Colc 3B 42 (4B 14)
Ballantyne Dr. CO2: Colc 6F 15
Ballast Quay Rd. CO5: Fing 6K 23
CO7: W'hoe 4A 24
BALLINGDON 5C 36
Ballingdon Gdns. CO10: Ball 5C 36
Ballingdon Gro. CO10: Ball 6D 36
Ballingdon Hill CO10: Ball 7B 36
Ballingdon Hill Ind. Est. CO10: Ball 5C 36
Ballingdon St. CO10: Ball 5C 36
Ballingdon Trad. Est. CO10: Ball 5D 36
Ball La. CO2: Colc 7B 22
Ball's Chase CO9: Hals 4C 38
BALLS GREEN 6K 17
Balmoral Av. CO15: Clac S 1G 35
Balton Way CO12: Har 5E 26
Banham Dr. CO10: Sud 3F 37
Banister Cl. CO16: Clac S 6F 31
Bank Bldgs. CO10: Sud 4E 36
Bank Pas. CO1: Colc 5A 42 (4A 14)
Bannatyne Health Club
Colchester 1F 23
Barbel Rd. CO4: Colc 2H 15
Barbour Gdns. CO2: Colc 2F 21
Barbrook La. CO5: Tip 4G 39
Barclay Sq. CO15: Jay 5D 34
Bardfield Rd. CO2: Colc 3C 22
Bardfield Way CO13: Frin S 4D 28
Bardsley Cl. CO4: Colc 1A 14
Barfield Rd. CO5: W Mer 5C 40
Barker Cl. CO11: Law 3D 10
Barker Rd. CO10: Sud 1E 36
Barkstead Rd. CO4: Colc 2E 14
Barley Cl. CO11: Mist 3H 11
Barley Ct. CO7: W'hoe 1A 24
Barley Way CO3: S'way 6D 12
Barlon Rd. CO7: Gt Bro, L Bro 7K 9
Barnardiston Rd. CO4: Colc 2E 14
Barncroft Cl. CO4: Colc 7D 6
Barnfield CO11: Mann 3F 11
Barnfield Rd. CO6: Gt Hork 4J 5
Barn Flds. CO3: S'way 5C 12
Barn Hall Av. CO2: Colc 7D 14
Barn La. CO11: L Bro 3J 9
Baronia Cft. CO4: Colc 7E 6
Baronswood Way CO2: Colc 2J 21
Barrack La. CO12: Har 3K 27
Barrack St. CO1: Colc 5D 14
Barr Cl. CO7: W'hoe 3A 24
Barrell Cl. CO7: Frat 1K 25
Barrington Cl. CO16: L Cla 1F 31
Barrington Gdns. CO15: Clac S 6B 32
Barrington Ho. CO2: Colc 6C 14
Barrington Rd. CO2: Colc 6C 14
Barrow M. CO5: W Mer 4E 40
Bartholomew Ct. CO4: Colc 7K 5
BASKETS 6J 19
Bassingham Cres. CO5: Tip 5J 39
Bateman Rd. CO7: B'sea 4G 41
BATH SIDE 2J 27
Bath St. CO7: W'hoe 4K 23
Bathurst Cl. CO2: Colc 3C 22
Battalion Wlk. CO2: Colc 7D 42 (6C 14)
Batt Hall CO10: Bulm 5B 36
Battisford Dr. CO16: Clac S 7D 30
Battlesbrook Rd. CO2: Colc 2F 23
Bawdsey Cl. CO16: Clac S 1E 34
Bawtree Way CO3: Colc 6G 13
Bayard Av. CO7: B'sea 5H 41
Baynard Grn. CO2: Colc 7B 14
Baynards Cres. CO13: Kir C 4C 28
Bay Rd. CO12: Har 3J 27
Bays Dr. CO9: Hals 3B 38
Bay Tree Cl. CO2: Colc 3K 21
Bay Vw. Cres. CO12: L Oak, R'sy 7B 26
Beach Cres. CO15: Jay 6C 34
Beachcroft Av. CO13: Kir C 4B 28
Beach Rd. CO5: W Mer 5C 40
CO12: Har 4H 27
CO15: Clac S 2J 35
Beach Way CO15: Jay 6C 34
Beacon Cl. CO7: B'sea 6G 41
BEACON END 5C 12
Beacon Hill Av. CO12: Har 3K 27
Beaconsfield Av. CO3: Colc 7A 42 (5A 14)
Beaconsfield Cl. CO10: Sud 3E 36
Beaconsfield Rd. CO10: Sud 3E 36
CO15: Clac S 1J 35
Beacon Way CO3: S'way 5C 12
Beatrice Rd. CO14: Walt 7H 29
CO15: Clac S 2H 35

Beatty Rd. CO10: Sud 2G 37
Beaumont Av. CO7: B'sea 5J 41
CO15: Clac S 1G 35
Beaumont Cl. CO4: Colc 6A 6
CO14: Walt 3D 28
Beaumonts, The CO13: Gt Hol 4A 28
Beaver Cl. CO3: Colc 4E 12
Beche Ho. CO2: Colc 7A 14
Beche Rd. CO2: Colc 6D 14
Becker Rd. CO3: Colc 7E 12
Beckford Cl. CO11: Mist 3J 11
Becontree Cl. CO15: Clac S 3J 31
Bedford Cl. CO5: Tip 5H 39
Bedford Rd. CO4: Colc 6B 6
CO15: Hol S 6B 32
Beech Av. CO7: W'hoe 3K 23
CO9: Hals 3D 38
Beech Gro. CO12: L Oak 7A 26
Beech Hill CO3: Colc 5G 13
Beech Rd. CO10: Gt Cor 5H 37
Beechwood Cl. CO2: Colc 2K 21
Beehive Ct. CO1: Colc 7E 42
Beeleigh Cl. CO2: Colc 3C 22
Begonia Pl. CO16: Clac S 7F 31
Belgrave Pl. CO1: Colc 4D 42 (4C 14)
Bellamy Cl. CO13: Kir C 4B 28
Belle Ct. CO15: Clac S 2H 35
Belle Vue Rd. CO1: Colc 1A 42 (2A 14)
CO7: W'hoe 4K 23
CO10: Sud 4F 37
Belle Vue Ter. CO9: Hals 3B 38
Bellfield Av. CO7: B'sea 4H 41
Bellfield Cl. CO7: B'sea 4J 41
Bell Grn. CO7: B'sea 5J 41
Bellingham Dr. CO6: Cop 1J 19
Bell Twr., The CO3: S'way 5D 12
(off New Farm Rd.)
Belmans Ct. CO12: Har 5E 26
Belmont Cres. CO4: Colc 7E 6
Belmont Pl. CO2: Colc 6E 14
Belsize Av. CO15: Jay 6A 34
Bembridge Cl. CO15: Clac S 3J 31
Bemerton Ct. CO13: Kir C 4A 28
Bemerton Gdns. CO13: Kir C 4A 28
Bendalls Ct. CO11: Law 3F 11
Benedict Ho. CO2: Colc 7A 14
Benhall Cl. CO16: Clac S 7D 30
Bennett Cl. CO14: Walt 2E 28
Bennett Ct. CO4: Colc 5G 15
Bennett Grn. CO4: Colc 4D 6
Bensusan Ct. CO2: Colc 1H 21
(off Iceni Way)
Bentall Cl. CO9: Hals 5C 38
Bentfield Ct. CO1: Colc 4E 14
Bentley Av. CO15: Jay 6B 34
Berberis Wlk. CO4: Colc 4G 15
BERECHURCH 3C 22
Berechurch Rd. CO2: Colc 3K 21
Berefield Way CO2: Colc 3B 22
Bergholt Rd. CO4: Colc 1K 13
CO6: For, W Ber 3A 4
CO11: Brant 1D 10
Beridge M. CO9: Hals 3A 38
Beridge Rd. CO9: Hals 3A 38
Beriffe Pl. CO7: B'sea 5H 41
Berkeley Rd. CO15: Clac S 7H 31
Berkley Cl. CO4: Colc 6E 6
Bernard Cl. CO13: Kir C 4C 28
Berrimans Cl. CO4: Colc 5F 15
Berryfield Cotts. CO1: Colc 4D 14
Berryfields CO1: Colc 4D 14
Bertram Av. CO16: L Cla 2G 31
Beryl Rd. CO12: Har 5C 26
Beth Av. CO7: W'hoe 5K 23
Beth Chatto Gdns. 6F 17
Betty Cocker Gro. CO10: Sud 4H 37
Beverley Av. CO5: W Mer 4E 40
Beverley Dr. CO13: Kir C 3C 28
Beverley Rd. CO3: Colc 5K 13
Bexhill Cl. CO15: Clac S 4F 35
Bexley Av. CO12: Har 6E 26
Bignell Ct. CO4: Colc 6E 6
Bijou Cl. CO5: Tip 4H 39
Bilsdale Cl. CO4: Colc 6E 6
BIRCH 7A 20
Birch Av. CO12: Har 4G 27
Birch Cl. CO7: B'sea 6G 41
CO15: Clac S 1F 35
Birch Dr. CO9: Hals 3D 38
Birches, The CO13: Kir C 4C 28

Birch Rd. CO2: Lay H 7D 20
CO6: Cop 6J 19
Birch St. CO2: B'ch 7A 20
Birchwood Cl. CO5: Tip 5J 39
CO5: W Mer 5D 40
Birchwood Way CO5: Tip 5K 39
Bird La. CO5: Tip 6J 39
Birkin Cl. CO5: Tip 6F 39
Bishop Rd. CO2: Colc 1G 21
Bishops Cl. CO10: Sud 1D 36
Bishops La. CO5: Tip 3G 39
Bisley Cl. CO16: Clac S 5E 30
Blackberry Rd. CO3: S'way 7C 12
Black Boy Yd. CO10: Sud 4E 36
Blackbrooke Cotts. CO6: Gt Hork 1J 5
Blackbrook Rd. CO6: Gt Hork 3J 5
Black Buoy Hill CO7: W'hoe 5K 23
Blackfriars CO10: Sud 5D 36
BLACKHEATH 4C 22
Blackheath CO2: Colc 4C 22
Blackhouse La. CO10: Gt Cor, L Cor 7J 37
Blacksmith's La. CO12: Har 4E 26
Blackthorn Av. CO4: Colc 4G 15
Blackthorn Rd. CO12: Har 4E 26
Blackthorns CO9: Hals 4A 38
Blackwater Av. CO4: Colc 1G 15
Blackwater Dr. CO5: W Mer 5A 40
Blade Rd. CO4: Colc 1J 13
Bladon Cl. CO5: Tip 5J 39
Blaine Dr. CO13: Kir C 3C 28
Blake Cl. CO11: Law 3D 10
Blake Dr. CO16: Clac S 5G 31
Blamsters Cres. CO9: Hals 5A 38
Blenheim Dr. CO2: Colc 4C 22
Blenheim Rd. CO15: Clac S 2G 35
Blenheim Way CO5: Tip 5J 39
Blind La. CO6: Eig G 3A 12
CO7: B'sea 5H 41
Bloom Cl. CO13: Frin S 4D 28
Bloomfield Av. CO13: Kir C 3C 28
Bloomsbury M. CO4: Colc 1K 13
Blossom M. CO5: W Mer 5D 40
Bloyes M. CO1: Colc 1B 42 (2B 14)
Bluebell Cl. CO16: Clac S 7F 31
Bluebell Way CO4: Colc 1J 13
Bluebottle Grove 5G 13
Bluebridge Cotts. CO9: Hals 4D 38
Bluebridge Ind. Est. CO9: Hals 4E 38
Bluehouse Av. CO16: Clac S 7D 30
Blue Rd. CO5: Tip 5G 39
Blyford Rd. CO16: Clac S 7D 30
Blythe Ct. CO7: W'hoe 4K 23
(off Station Rd.)
Blyths La. CO7: W'hoe 4K 23
(off High St.)
Boadicea Way CO2: Colc 7H 13
Boarded Barn Rd. CO6: Cop 6H 19
Boat Ho., The CO7: B'sea 7G 41
Bobbits Way CO7: W'hoe 4A 24
Bober Ct. CO2: Colc 5D 22
BOCKING'S ELM 5F 31
Bocking's Gro. CO16: Clac S 6E 30
Bois Fld. Ter. CO9: Hals 3C 38
Bois Hall Gdns. CO9: Hals 2C 38
Bokhara Cl. CO5: Tip 4G 39
Boley Dr. CO15: Clac S 7K 31
Boleyn Way CO15: Jay 4C 34
Bolls La. CO2: Lay H 7E 20
Bolsin Dr. CO4: Colc 6A 6
Bonham Ct. CO15: Clac S 7H 31
Bonners Saltings (Nature Reserve) 1B 40
Booth Av. CO4: Colc 4E 14
Borehamgate CO10: Sud 4F 37
(off King St.)
Borges Gdns. CO4: Colc 6K 5
BORLEY 1A 36
Boscombe Ct. CO15: Hol S 5E 32
Botany La. CO16: Clac S, St O 1A 34
Boudicca Wlk. CO7: W'hoe 1A 24
Boundary Rd. CO4: Colc 6G 15
Bounstead Hill CO2: Lay H 7J 21
Bounstead Rd. CO2: Colc 6K 21
Bourchier Way CO9: Hals 5A 38
Bourne Cl. CO9: Hals 5A 38
Bourne Ct. CO2: Colc 7C 14
Bourne Mill 7D 14
Bournemouth Rd. CO15: Hol S 5E 32
Bourne Rd. CO2: Colc 7C 14
CO6: W Ber 7D 4
Bower Gro. CO5: W Mer 3E 40
Bower Hall La. CO5: W Mer 2E 40
Bowes Rd. CO7: W'hoe 3A 24
Box Mill La. CO9: Hals 2B 38
Boxted Airfield Mus. 1E 6
Boxted Av. CO16: Clac S 6E 30

Boxted Rd.—Castle Bailey

Boxted Rd. CO4: Boxt, Colc 5K **5**
Boyles Ct. CO2: Colc 5D **22**
Brackens, The CO4: Colc 7D **6**
Bradbrook Cotts. CO6: W Ber 6F **5**
Bradford Dr. CO4: Colc 1A **14**
Brading Av. CO15: Clac S 4K **31**
Bradman Ct. CO2: Colc 7B **42** (6B **14**)
Braeburn Rd. CO6: Gt Hork 3H **5**
Braemore Cl. CO4: Colc 7F **7**
BRAISWICK 1J **13**
Braiswick CO4: Colc 7H **5**
Braiswick La. CO4: Colc 6K **5**
Braiswick Pl. CO4: Colc 7J **5**
Braithwaite Dr. CO4: Colc 1A **14**
Brambledown CO5: W Mer 4C **40**
Brambles CO14: Walt 3E **28**
Brambles, The CO3: Colc 1F **21**
Bramble Tye CO12: Har 6C **26**
Bramble Way CO15: Clac S 4J **31**
Bramley Cl. CO3: Colc 4H **13**
CO7: Alr 4F **25**
Brands Cl. CO10: Gt Cor 6K **37**
Branscombe Cl. CO13: Frin S 5C **28**
Branston Rd. CO15: Clac S 1F **35**
Braybrooke M. CO10: Ball 5C **36**
Breakmoor Hill CO10: Midd 7E **36**
Bream Ct. CO4: Colc 2H **15**
Bree Av. CO6: M Tey 3C **18**
Breeze La. CO4: Colc 1H **13**
Brendon Ct. CO5: Tip 6H **39**
Brendon Dr. CO9: Hals 5C **38**
Brent Cl. CO13: Kir C 3D **28**
Brentwood Rd. CO15: Hol S 5B **32**
Bretten Cl. CO16: Clac S 7D **30**
Bretts Bldgs. CO1: Colc 6E **42** (5C **14**)
Brewery Dr. CO9: Hals 5B **38**
Brewery Twr., The CO1: Colc 4E **42**
Brewster Cl. CO9: Hals 5C **38**
Brian Bishop Cl. CO14: Walt 2F **29**
Briardale Av. CO12: Har 4E **26**
Briarfields CO13: Kir S 2A **28**
Briar Rd. CO7: Gt Bro 6F **9**
Briarwood Av. CO15: Hol S 5E **32**
Briarwood End CO4: Colc 7D **6**
Brickhouse Cl. CO5: W Mer 4B **40**
Brick Kiln La. CO6: Gt Hork 4H **5**
CO7: Thorr 7J **25**
Brick Kiln Rd. CO1: Colc 1A **42** (2A **14**)
Brickmakers La. CO4: Colc 1B **14**
Brick St. CO3: Ford H 2B **12**
Bridgebrook Cl. CO4: Colc 2F **15**
Bridgefield Cl. CO4: Colc 4E **14**
Bridge Pl. CO11: Catt 1E **10**
Bridge St. CO9: Hals 3B **38**
Bridle Wlk. *CO3: S'way 5D 12*
(off Stirrup M.)
Bridleway, The CO3: Ford H 2A **12**
Brierley Av. CO5: W Mer 4E **40**
Brierley Paddock CO5: W Mer 4E **40**
Brigade Gro. CO2: Colc 6C **14**
Bright Cl. CO16: Clac S 5G **31**
BRIGHTLINGSEA 6H **41**
Brightlingsea Mus. 6H **41**
Brightlingsea Open Air Swimming Pool 7G **41**
Brightlingsea Rd.
CO7: B'sea, Thorr 2F **41**, 7K **25**
CO7: Elm M 6K **15**
Brightlingsea Sports Cen. 4G **41**
Brighton Rd. CO15: Hol S 5E **32**
Brightside CO13: Kir C 3C **28**
Brindley Rd. CO15: Clac S 3A **32**
Brinkley Cres. CO4: Colc 2F **15**
Brinkley Gro. Rd. CO4: Colc 5C **6**
Brinkley La. CO4: Colc 5D **6**
Brinkley Pl. CO4: Colc 7B **6**
Brisbane Way CO2: Colc 3C **22**
Bristol Rd. CO1: Colc 2E **42** (3C **14**)
Britannia Ct. CO7: W'hoe 3K **23**
Britannia Cres. CO7: W'hoe 3K **23**
Britannia M. CO2: Colc 7B **14**
Brittany Way CO2: Colc 7D **14**
Britten Cl. CO4: Colc 5G **15**
Britton Way CO15: Clac S 4G **31**
Brixham Cl. CO15: Clac S 4F **35**
Broadfields CO7: W'hoe 7A **16**
Broadlands Way CO4: Colc 2D **14**
Broad La. CO6: Boxt, Gt Hork 1H **5**
Broad Lanes CO7: Elm M 7C **16**
Broadmead Rd. CO4: Colc 2G **15**
Broadmere Cl. CO15: Hol S 4D **32**
Broad Oak La. CO4: Colc 1B **14**
Broad Oaks Pk. CO4: Colc 7F **7**
Broadway CO15: Jay 6C **34**
Brock Cl. CO5: Tip 4J **39**
Brockham Cl. CO16: Clac S 5E **30**
Bromley Cl. CO16: Clac S 7G **31**
BROMLEY CROSS 6F **9**
Bromley Hgts. CO4: Colc 3H **15**
Bromley Rd. CO4: Colc 2G **15**
CO7: A'lgh 2G **15**
CO7: Elm M 6E **16**
CO7: Frat 7K **17**
CO11: Law, L Bro 5C **10**
Bronze Ct. CO9: Hals 4B **38**
Brook Cl. CO5: Tip 7K **39**
Brookdale Ct. CO1: Colc 6E **42**
Brook Farm Cl. CO9: Hals 4E **38**
Brook Hall Rd. CO5: Fing 6K **23**
Brookland CO5: Tip 6G **39**
Brooklands CO1: Colc 6E **42** (5C **14**)
CO15: Jay 6B **34**
Brooklands Gdns. CO15: Jay 6B **34**
Brook Lodge CO3: Colc 5J **13**
Brooklyn Ct. *CO12: Har 4H 27*
(off Brooklyn Rd.)
Brooklyn M. CO12: Har 4H **27**
Brooklyn Rd. CO12: Har 4H **27**
Brook Mdws. CO5: Tip 5G **39**
Brook Pl. CO9: Hals 4B **38**
Brook Retail Pk. CO15: Clac S 4H **31**
Brook Rd. CO5: Tip, Tol K 7K **39**
CO6: Aldh, M Tey 1F **10**
Brookside Cl. CO2: Colc 7D **14**
Brooks Malting CO11: Mann 3F **11**
Brook St. CO1: Colc 4D **14**
CO7: Gt Bro 2J **17**
CO7: W'hoe 4K **23**
CO11: Mann 3F **11**
Broome Gro. CO7: W'hoe 2K **23**
Broome Way CO15: Jay 6C **34**
Broomfield Cres. CO7: W'hoe 2K **23**
Broomfield Rd. CO7: Elm M 7G **17**
Broom Hill CO9: Hals 3C **38**
Broomhills Rd. CO5: W Mer 5D **40**
Broom St. CO10: Gt Cor 6H **37**
Broton Dr. CO9: Hals 3B **38**
(not continuous)
Brougham Glades CO3: S'way 6D **12**
Broughton Cl. CO2: Colc 7J **13**
Browning Cl. CO3: Colc 5F **13**
Brownsea Way CO3: Colc 7G **13**
Bruff Cl. CO4: Colc 1A **14**
Bruff Dr. CO14: Walt 3E **28**
Bruges Cl. CO12: Har 6F **27**
Brundells Rd. CO7: Gt Bro 6K **17**
BRUNDON 2C **36**
Brundon La. CO10: Ball, Sud 5C **36**
Brunel Bus. Cen. CO15: Clac S 3A **32**
Brunel Ct. CO4: Colc 4E **6**
Brunel Ct. Ind. Est. CO4: Colc 5E **6**
Brunel Rd. CO15: Clac S 3A **32**
Brunel Way CO4: Colc 4E **6**
Brunswick Ho. Cut CO11: Mist 4J **11**
Brussels Cl. CO12: Har 6G **27**
Bryanstone M. CO3: Colc 6E **12**
Buckfast Av. CO13: Kir C 4B **28**
Buckingham Dr. CO4: Colc 4G **15**
Buddleia Ct. CO7: W'hoe 2J **23**
Buffett Way CO4: Colc 5G **15**
Buick Av. CO15: Jay 6A **34**
Builder Gdns. CO2: Colc 3B **22**
Bullace Cl. CO4: Colc 7F **7**
Bullfinch Cl. CO4: Colc 3H **15**
CO12: Har 6D **26**
Bullfinch Dr. CO9: Hals 4D **38**
Bull Hill Rd. CO15: Clac S 6J **31**
Bull La. CO5: Tip 6G **39**
Bullocks La. CO10: Sud 4E **36**
Bullocks Ter. CO10: Sud 5E **36**
Bullock Wood Cl. CO4: Colc 6F **7**
Bulmer Rd. CO10: Ball 5C **36**
Bulmer Rd. Ind. Est. CO10: Ball 4C **36**
Buntingford Ct. CO2: Colc 3C **22**
Bures Rd. CO6: L Hork, W Ber 2C **4**
CO10: Gt Cor 5G **37**
Burgate Cl. CO16: Clac S 7D **30**
Burkitts La. CO10: Sud 4E **36**
Burlington Rd. CO3: Colc 6A **42** (5A **14**)
Burmanny Cl. CO15: Clac S 1F **35**
Burnham Cl. CO14: Walt 2F **29**
Burnham Ct. CO15: Clac S 4F **35**
Burns Av. CO3: Colc 5F **13**
BURNT HEATH 6F **9**
Burr Cl. CO12: R'sy 6B **26**
Burroughs Piece Rd. CO10: Sud 4F **37**
Burrows Cl. CO11: Law 3D **10**
CO16: Clac S 5G **31**
Burrs Rd. CO15: Clac S 6J **31**
Burrsville M. CO15: Clac S 4K **31**
BURRSVILLE PARK 4K **31**
Burstall Cl. CO16: Clac S 7E **30**
Bury Cl. CO1: Colc 3E **42** (3C **14**)
CO6: M Tey 2D **18**
Burywoods CO4: Colc 7H **5**
Bushell Way CO13: Kir C 4C **28**
Bush Gro. CO10: Ball 5C **36**
Butchers La. CO14: Walt 3F **29**
Butler Rd. CO9: Hals 3A **38**
Butt Rd. CO2: Colc 7A **42** (6K **13**)
CO3: Colc 7A **42** (6K **13**)
CO10: Gt Cor 5H **37**
Buxey Cl. CO5: W Mer 4B **40**
Buxton Rd. CO2: Colc 1C **22**
Byford Rd. CO10: Sud 2G **37**
Byng Ct. CO2: Colc 3C **22**
Byron Av. CO3: Colc 4F **13**
Byron's Yd. CO1: Colc 4A **42**

C

Cabbage Hall La. CO2: Colc 4D **22**
Cadenhouse M. CO3: Colc 4E **12**
Caelum Dr. CO2: Colc 6F **15**
Cairns Rd. CO2: Colc 2C **22**
California Cl. CO4: Colc 6D **6**
California Rd. CO11: Mist 3J **11**
Cambie Cres. CO4: Colc 6A **6**
Cambrai Rd. CO2: Colc 7K **13**
Cambria Cl. CO11: Mist 4K **11**
Cambridge Ct. CO15: Clac S 7H **31**
Cambridge Rd. CO3: Colc 6J **13**
CO13: Frin S 5E **28**
CO15: Clac S 7H **31**
Cambridge Wlk. CO3: Colc 6K **13**
Camellia Av. CO16: Clac S 7F **31**
Camellia Ct. CO4: Colc 3F **15**
Camellia Cres. CO16: Clac S 6F **31**
Camomile Way CO4: Colc 1J **13**
Campbell Ct. CO3: Colc 5K **13**
Campbell Dr. CO4: Colc 1G **15**
Campernell Cl. CO7: B'sea 4H **41**
Camp Folley Nth. CO2: Colc 7C **42** (5B **14**)
Camp Folley Sth. CO2: Colc 6C **14**
Campion Rd. CO2: Colc 6C **14**
Camp Rd. CO7: Gt Bro 4K **17**
Camulodunum Way CO2: Colc 3J **21**
Camulus Cl. CO2: Colc 2G **21**
Canberra Cl. CO2: Colc 3C **22**
Canhams Rd. CO10: Gt Cor 6H **37**
Cann Cl. CO10: Sud 1D **36**
Canning St. CO12: Har 2J **27**
Cannon Rd. CO1: Colc 5D **14**
Cannons, The CO2: Colc 7J **13**
Cannons Cl. CO2: Colc 7K **13**
Cannon St. CO1: Colc 5D **14**
Canterbury Rd. CO2: Colc 6C **14**
CO10: Sud 1D **36**
CO15: Hol S 6D **32**
Canters Mdw. Ct. CO15: Clac S 6K **31**
Canwick Gro. CO2: Colc 7E **14**
Cape Cl. CO3: Colc 6F **13**
Capel Pk. CO13: Kir C 3C **28**
Capel Rd. CO3: Colc 6J **13**
Capon Rd. CO4: Colc 6G **15**
Cap Pillar Cl. CO7: W'hoe 2K **23**
Capstan Pl. CO4: Colc 6F **15**
Captain Gdns. CO2: Colc 6C **14**
Captains Rd. CO5: W Mer 5B **40**
Caracalla Way CO4: Colc 4C **6**
Carbonels CO10: Gt Wal 1K **37**
Cardinal Cl. CO4: Colc 4H **15**
Carisbrooke Av. CO15: Clac S 3K **31**
Carleton Ct. CO5: Rhdge 4G **23**
Carlisle Cl. CO1: Colc 2E **42** (3C **14**)
Carlton M. CO7: W'hoe 4J **23**
Carlton Rd. CO15: Clac S 6A **32**
Carnarvon Rd. CO15: Clac S 1J **35**
Carolina Way CO5: Tip 4H **39**
Caroline Cl. CO7: W'hoe 1A **24**
Caroline Ct. CO3: Colc 1G **21**
Carolyn Ct. CO2: Colc 7E **14**
Carriers Cl. CO5: W Mer 4A **40**
Carrington Ct. CO5: W Mer 4D **40**
Carrington Ho. CO5: W Mer 4D **40**
Carringtons Rd. CO7: Gt Bro 6F **9**
Carrs Rd. CO15: Clac S 1G **35**
Carshalton End CO3: Colc 7F **13**
Carsons Dr. CO10: Gt Cor 6J **37**
Cartbridge Cl. CO14: Walt 2F **29**
Carters Cl. CO16: Clac S 1E **34**
Carters Ct. CO1: Colc 6E **42**
Carus Cres. CO4: Colc 5C **6**
Cassino Rd. CO2: Colc 1J **21**
Castle Bailey CO1: Colc 4C **42** (4B **14**)

Castle Ct. CO1: Colc 3B 42
CO15: Clac S 1H 35
Castle Folley CO1: Colc 3C 42 (3B 14)
Castlegate St. CO12: Har 1K 27
Castle Hill Pk. CO16: Clac S 4H 31
Castle Rd. CO1: Colc 3D 42 (3C 14)
CO15: Clac S 1H 35
Castleward Cl. CO7: W'hoe 4A 24
Catchpole Ct. CO10: Sud 4E 36
Catchpool Rd. CO1: Colc 1B 42 (2B 14)
Caterham Cl. CO16: Clac S 5F 31
Cater Wlk. CO4: Colc 4C 6
Catesby Mdw. CO10: Sud 5D 36
Catherine Cl. CO15: Clac S 6K 31
Catherine Hunt Way CO2: Colc 2H 21
Catkin M. CO2: Colc 3J 21
Cat's La. CO10: Sud 5G 37
CATTAWADE 1E 10
Cattawade St. CO11: Catt 1E 10
Cattermole Cl. CO16: Clac S 1E 34
Causeway, The CO4: Colc 2E 14
CO6: Gt Hork 1H 5
CO9: Hals 4B 38
CO11: Catt .1D 10
Causeway End CO11: Law 2D 10
Causeway Reach CO15: Clac S 4H 31
Causton Rd. CO1: Colc 2A 42 (3A 14)
Caustons Cl. CO10: Gt Cor 6J 37
Cavalier Gro. CO2: Colc 6C 14
Cavalry Rd. CO2: Colc 7A 42 (6A 14)
Cavendish Av. CO2: Colc 7E 14
Cavendish Dr. CO11: Law 4D 10
CO16: Clac S 7D 30
Cavendish Way CO10: Sud 3F 37
Caxton Cl. CO5: Tip 6H 39
Caxton Ct. CO4: Colc 4E 6
Cedar Av. CO5: Tip 3G 39
CO7: B'sea .5G 41
Cedar Cl. CO14: Walt 3E 28
Cedar Ct. CO6: W Ber 5D 4
Cedar Cres. CO11: Law 4E 10
Cedar M. CO16: Clac S 6F 31
Cedars Rd. CO2: Colc 6B 42 (5B 14)
Celandine Ct. CO4: Colc 1J 13
Celia Wlk. CO4: Colc 4H 15
(off Hamlet Dr.)
Centaury Cl. CO3: S'way 4C 12
Centenary Way CO16: Clac S, L Cla 2G 31
Central Av. CO13: Frin S 4E 28
Central Maltings, The CO11: Mann 3F 11
Centre, The CO4: Colc 4E 6
CO5: Tip 5H 39
CO9: Hals .3B 38
Centurion Ho. CO2: Colc 6B 42
Centurion Way CO2: Colc 2G 21
Century Cinema
Clacton-on-Sea 1H 35
Chaffinch Dr. CO12: Har 6D 26
Chaffinch Gdns. CO4: Colc 3H 15
Chaffinch Way CO9: Hals 4D 38
Chalfont Rd. CO4: Colc 1E 14
Challenge Way CO1: Colc 5D 14
Chamberlain Av. CO14: Walt 3F 29
Chancery Gro. CO2: Colc 4C 22
Chandlers Cl. CO5: W Mer 4C 40
CO16: Clac S 1E 34
Chandlers Row CO1: Colc 6E 14
Chaney Rd. CO7: W'hoe 2J 23
Chant Cl. CO4: Colc 7F 7
Chanterelle Ct. CO4: Colc 7D 6
Chantry, The CO3: Colc 4J 13
Chantry Cl. CO10: Sud 1D 36
CO16: Clac S 4H 31
Chapel Cft. CO5: A'lgh 3C 8
Chapel Cut CO11: Mist 3J 11
Chapelfields CO13: Kir C 4C 28
Chapel Hill CO9: Hals 3A 38
Chapel La. CO5: Tip 5J 39
CO6: W Ber 6E 4
CO7: Crock H 1K 15
CO7: Elm M 5E 16
Chapel Rd. CO3: S'way 5C 12
CO5: Fing .7G 23
CO5: Tip 6H 39
CO6: W Ber 7D 4
CO7: B'sea .6J 41
CO7: W'hoe 4K 23
Chapel St. CO5: Rhdge 4H 23
CO9: Hals .3B 38
Chapel St. Nth. CO2: Colc 6A 42 (5A 14)
Chapel St. Sth. CO2: Colc 6A 42 (5A 14)
Chaplin Dr. CO4: Colc 2F 15
Chaplins CO13: Kir C 3D 28
Chaplin Wlk. CO10: Gt Cor 6K 37
Chapman Pl. CO4: Colc 4D 6

Chapman Rd. CO15: Clac S 1J 35
Chariot Dr. CO2: Colc 1B 22
Charles Burcart Gdns. CO15: Clac S 7H 31
Charles Ct. CO3: S'way 5D 12
CO7: W'hoe 1A 24
Charles Ho. CO1: Colc 3B 42 (3B 14)
Charles May Ho. CO1: Colc 5A 42
Charles Pell Rd. CO4: Colc 5G 15
Charles Pl. CO1: Colc 5E 14
Charles Smith Ho. CO2: Colc 1C 22
(off Ladbrook Dr.)
Charles St. CO1: Colc 7E 42 (5C 14)
Charleston Ct. CO5: W Mer 5E 40
Charlotte Dr. CO13: Kir C 4C 28
Charnock Cl. CO13: Kir C 4D 28
Charter Ct. CO4: Colc 4E 6
Charter Way CO4: Colc 6B 6
Chartfield Dr. CO13: Kir S 2B 28
Chase, The CO1: Colc 4F 15
(Bentleigh Ct.)
CO1: Colc .4D 14
(East St.)
CO3: Colc .5E 12
CO4: Colc .4G 15
CO5: W Mer 5C 40
CO7: Elm M 5F 17
CO11: Mann 4F 11
CO15: Hol S 6D 32
Chase Ct. CO4: Colc 4G 15
Chase La. CO12: Har 5D 26
Chase Way, The CO3: Colc 3G 13
Chatsworth Gdns. CO15: Clac S 2G 35
Chatsworth Rd. CO5: W Mer 4C 40
Chaucer Cl. CO15: Jay 3D 34
Chaucer Rd. CO10: Sud 1D 36
Chaucer Way CO3: Colc, S'way 5F 13
Chelmer Cl. CO13: Kir C 3C 28
Chelmsford Rd. CO15: Hol S 6B 32
Chelsea Ct. CO10: Sud 4F 37
Chelsea Rd. CO10: Sud 4F 37
Chelsworth Av. CO10: Gt Cor 5H 37
Chelsworth Cl. CO10: Sud 5H 37
Chelston Ho. CO7: Alr 5E 24
Chequers Rd. CO11: L Bro, Mist 5E 10
Cherry Chase CO5: Tip 6H 39
Cherry Row CO3: Colc 6F 13
Cherry Tree Av. CO15: Clac S 3F 35
Cherry Tree Cl. CO9: Hals 3D 38
Cherrytree Cl. CO15: Clac S 6F 13
Cherry Tree La. CO2: Colc 6B 22
Cherrytree Rd. CO10: Gt Cor 4H 37
Cherrywood Dr. CO3: Colc 6F 13
Cherrywoods CO7: Alr 4F 25
Chervil Cl. CO5: Tip 6G 39
Chester Chalet & Cvn. Camp CO16: Clac S 7C 30
Chesterwell M. CO4: Colc 4K 5
Chestnut Av. CO2: Colc 4C 22
CO13: Kir C 4A 28
CO15: Clac S 1F 35
CO16: Clac S 2D 34
Chestnut Cl. CO4: Colc 5K 5
Chestnut M. CO10: Sud 4E 36
(off Friars St.)
Chestnut Rd. CO7: Alr 4F 25
Chestnut Way CO5: Tip 4G 39
CO7: B'sea .5G 41
Cheveling Rd. CO2: Colc 2F 23
Chevy Ct. CO12: R'sy 5B 26
Chilburn Gdns. CO15: Clac S 4K 31
Chilburn Rd. CO15: Clac S 4J 31
Childsplay Adventureland 1A 42 (2A 14)
Childwell All. CO1: Colc 6D 42 (5C 14)
(not continuous)
Chiltern Cl. CO1: Colc 2A 14
CHILTON 2H 37
Chilton Cl. CO6: Gt Hork 3H 5
Chilton Cnr. CO10: Gt Wal 1K 37
Chilton Ct. CO10: Sud 4G 37
Chilton Gro. CO10: Sud 1J 37
Chilton Ind. Est. CO10: Sud 3H 37
(not continuous)
Chilton Lodge Rd. CO10: Sud 4G 37
Chingford Av. CO15: Clac S 3J 31
Chinook CO4: Colc 6D 6
Chipping Hill CO9: Hals 3C 38
(off Head St.)
Chipstead Wlk. CO16: Clac S 5F 31
Chittock Cl. CO16: Clac S 1E 34
Chitts Hill CO3: Colc, S'way 1D 12
CHITTS HILLS 3D 12
Christ Church Ct. CO3: Colc 6J 13
Christine Chase CO3: Colc 6F 13
Christopher Ct. CO10: Sud 4E 36
(off Christopher La.)

Christopher Dr. CO16: L Cla 2G 31
Christopher La. CO10: Sud 4E 36
Church Cl. CO6: W Ber 6E 4
Church Cres. CO15: Clac S 2J 35
Church Farm Way CO4: Colc 6A 6
Churchfield Bus. Pk. CO10: Sud 2J 37
Church Fld. Rd. CO10: Sud 2H 37
Churchfield Rd. CO14: Walt 2G 29
Churchfields CO5: W Mer 5B 40
Churchfields Av. CO3: S'way 7C 12
Church Hill CO5: Rhdge 4H 23
CO11: Law .4B 10
CO12: R'sy .6A 26
Churchill Av. CO9: Hals 2C 38
Churchill Cl. CO7: B'sea 4H 41
Churchill Ct. CO12: Har 3F 27
Churchill Dr. CO10: Sud 1E 36
Churchill Rd. CO5: Tip 5K 39
Churchill Way CO2: Colc 7D 14
Church La. CO3: Colc 6F 13
CO3: S'way .6A 12
(not continuous)
CO6: L Tey, M Tey 3A 18
CO6: M Tey .2E 18
CO11: Mist .3G 11
CO12: Har .1K 27
CO13: Gt Hol 7A 28
Church M. CO5: Tip 5H 39
Church Mdw. CO2: Lay H 7F 21
CO5: Fing .7J 23
CO5: Tip 4G 39
CO5: W Mer 5B 40
CO6: Cop .4H 19
CO7: Alr 5F 25
CO7: B'sea .2F 41
CO7: Elm M 5E 16
CO7: Frat .1H 25
CO9: G'std G 7D 38
CO10: Bulm 7A 36
CO10: Gt Cor 6G 37
CO11: Bro, L Bro 6K 9
CO14: Walt 2G 29
CO15: Clac S 2J 35
Church St. CO1: Colc 5A 42 (4A 14)
CO5: Rhdge 4H 23
CO10: Sud .5D 36
CO12: Har .1J 27
Church Vw. CO7: A'lgh 3C 8
Church Vw. Cl. CO9: Hals 5B 38
CO10: Sud .4E 36
Churchwell Av. CO5: Ethpe 7E 18
Churnwood Cl. CO4: Colc 2F 15
Churnwood Rd. CO4: Colc 2F 15
Cinque Port Rd. CO7: B'sea 5H 41
Circular Rd. E. CO2: Colc 7B 42 (6B 14)
(not continuous)
Circular Rd. Nth. CO2: Colc 7A 42 (6A 14)
Circular Rd. Sth. CO2: Colc 7A 14
Circular Rd. W. CO2: Colc 6A 14
Circus Sq. CO2: Colc 1B 22
Cistern Yd. CO1: Colc 4A 42 (4A 14)
City Rd. CO5: W Mer 5A 40
CLACTON & DISTRICT HOSPITAL 3H 35
Clacton Factory Shop. Village
CO15: Clac S 2K 31
Clacton Leisure Cen. 7J 31
CLACTON-ON-SEA 2J 35
Clacton-on-Sea Golf Course 4F 35
Clacton-on-Sea Sailing Club 5F 33
Clacton-on-Sea Station (Rail) 1J 35
Clacton Pier 3J 35
Clacton Rd. CO7: Elm M 6K 15
(not continuous)
CO7: Thorr .7K 25
CO11: Hor X, Mist 4F 11
CO13: Gt Hol 5E 32
CO15: Hol S 5E 32
CO16: St O .7A 30
Clairmont Rd. CO3: Colc 6E 12
Clapgate Dr. CO16: L Cla 1F 31
Clara Reeve Cl. CO3: Colc 7F 13
Clare Cl. CO9: Hals 5A 38
Claremont Hgts. CO1: Colc 1A 42 (2A 14)
Claremont Rd. CO7: W'hoe 4A 24
Clarence Rd. CO10: Sud 3E 36
Clarendon Pk. CO15: Clac S 6A 32
Clarendon Way CO1: Colc 1A 42 (2A 14)
Clare Way CO16: Clac S 6E 30
Clarice House Day Spa
Colchester .4G 21
Clarkesmead CO5: Tip 6G 39
Clarke's Rd. CO12: Har 4E 26
Clarkia Wlk. CO4: Colc 4F 15
Claude Oliver Cl. CO11: Law 5C 10

Claudius Ct. CO1: Colc 3B 42
Claudius Rd. CO2: Colc 6C 14
Clayhall Rd. CO15: Clac S 6K 31
Clay La. CO16: St O 4A 30
Clay La. Gro. CO4: Colc 6F 7
Clays Rd. CO14: Walt 2E 28
Clayton Rd. CO12: R'sy 5B 26
Clear Springs CO12: Har 6F 27
Clearwater CO2: Colc 7D 14
Cleave Cl. CO4: Clac S 5E 30
Clematis Way CO4: Colc 4G 15
Clement Mellish Ct. CO1: Colc 4B 42
Clermont Av. CO10: Sud 1D 36
Cleveland Cl. CO4: Colc 6E 6
Clibbon Ct. CO10: Gt Cor 5H 37
Cliff Ct. CO12: Har 4J 27
    CO13: Frin S 4F 29
Cliff Pde. CO14: Walt 7J 29
Cliff Rd. CO12: Har 4H 27
    CO15: Hol S 6D 32
Cliff Way CO13: Frin S 5F 29
Clifton Ct. CO14: Walt 3G 29
Clifton Ter. CO7: W'hoe 4K 23
Clear La. CO15: Clac S 6E 30
    CO16: Clac S 6E 30
Clo'x.ers, The CO10: Sud 2H 37
Close, The CO10: Sud 3F 37
    CO12: Har 4F 27
    CO13: Frin S 5C 28
    CO15: Jay 5E 34
Clough Rd. CO4: Colc 4F 7
Clover Ct. CO3: S'way 6D 12
    CO10: Gt Cor 5J 37
Cloverlands CO4: Colc 1E 14
Clovers CO9: Hals 4A 38
Clover Way CO7: A'lgh 5K 7
Coach Rd. CO6: Gt Hork 2E 4
    CO7: Alr 5F 25
Coan Av. CO15: Clac S 3G 35
Coast Rd. CO5: W Mer 4A 40
Coats Hutton Rd. CO16: 1H 21
Cobble Row CO3: S'way 5D 12
Cobbold Ho. CO12: Har 3F 27
Cockaynes La. CO7: Alr 3E 24
Cockett Wick La. CO16: St O 3A 34
Coeur de Lion CO4: Colc 1B 14
Coggeshall Pieces CO9: Hals 3D 38
Coggeshall Rd. CO6: Cogg, M Tey 3A 18
    CO7: A'lgh, Ded 1D 8
Coggeshall Way CO9: Hals 3D 38
Cohort Dr. CO2: Colc 2G 21
Coke St. CO12: Har 2J 27
COLCHESTER 5B 42 (4A 14)
Colchester Academy Sports Cen.
    ....3G 15
Colchester & East Sussex Cricket Club
    ....2C 42 (3B 14)
Colchester Art Cen. 5A 42 (4A 14)
Colchester Bus. Pk. CO4: Colc 4E 6
Colchester Bus Station 6C 42 (5B 14)
Colchester By-Pass CO3: Colc 3H 13
Colchester By-Pass Rd. CO1: Colc 1C 42 (2C 14)
    CO4: Colc 5G 15
Colchester Camping & Cvn. Pk. CO3: .3F 13
Colchester Castle Mus. 4C 42 (4B 14)
Colchester Crematorium CO2: Colc 1B 22
Colchester Garrison Athletics Stadium 6A 14
COLCHESTER GENERAL HOSPITAL 7B 6
Colchester Golf Course 7J 5
Colchester Main Rd. CO7: Alr 2E 24
Colchester Natural History Mus. ...5C 42 (4B 14)
Colchester (Park & Ride) 3A 6
Colchester Retail Pk. CO3: Colc 4K 13
Colchester Rd. CO5: Tip 3H 39
    CO5: W Mer 4C 40
    CO6: L Hork, Wmgfd 1A 4
    CO6: W Ber 5E 4
    CO7: A'lgh 5A 8
                        (Harwich Rd.)
    CO7: A'lgh 7H 7
                     (Parson's Heath)
    CO7: A'lgh, Gt Bro 7D 8
    CO7: Elm M 5C 16
    CO7: Frat 1K 25
    CO7: W'hoe 6J 15
    CO9: Hals 3C 38
    CO11: Law 4D 10
    CO15: Hol S 6B 32
Colchester Station (Rail) 1A 42 (2A 14)
Colchester Town Station (Rail) 6D 42 (5C 14)
Colchester United FC 4A 6
Colchester Zoo 4B 20
Cold Hall Chase CO7: Gt Bro 5J 17
Cole Dr. CO10: Gt Cor 6J 37
Coleman Ct. CO15: Clac S 1J 35
Coles La. CO14: Walt 2E 28

Colet Cres. CO2: Colc 7B 14
College Ct. CO11: Law 3E 10
College Rd. CO15: Clac S 1K 35
Coller Rd. CO12: Har 2E 26
Collindale Gdns. CO15: Clac S 6B 32
Collingwood Grn. CO15: Clac S 3G 35
Collingwood Rd. CO3: Colc 5E 12
    CO15: Clac S 3G 35
Collyers Ct. CO1: Colc 4D 14
                            (off East St.)
Colne, The CO7: B'sea 7G 41
Colne Bank Av. CO1: Colc 1A 42 (3K 13)
    CO3: Colc 3K 13
Colne C'way. CO2: Colc 6F 15
Colne Engaine Rd. CO9: Hals 1D 38
Colne Ri. CO5: Rhdge 4H 23
Colne Rd. CO7: B'sea 6G 41
    CO9: Hals 3C 38
    CO15: Clac S 2J 35
Colne Ter. CO7: W'hoe 4K 23
Colne Valley Cl. CO9: Hals 3A 38
Colneys Cl. CO10: Sud 2D 36
Colthorpe Rd. CO15: Clac S 3J 31
Coltsfoot Ct. CO4: Colc 1J 13
Columbine Cen., The
    Walton-on-the-Naze 1H 29
Columbine Gdns. CO4: Walt 3F 29
Columbine M. CO3: S'way 4C 12
Colvin Cl. CO3: Colc 4F 13
Commerce Pk. CO2: Colc 7F 15
Commerce Way CO2: Colc 7F 15
    CO11: Law 2E 10
Commons, The CO3: Colc 6F 13
Compton M. CO4: Colc 3E 14
Compton Rd. CO4: Colc 3D 14
Comyns Cl. CO4: Colc 4C 6
Conder Way CO2: Colc 7E 14
Coney Byes La. CO6: W Ber 3C 4
Congregational Ho. CO9: Hals 3C 38
                        (off Parsonage St.)
Conies Rd. CO9: Hals 5A 38
Conifer Cl. CO4: Colc 3F 15
    CO7: Alr 5D 24
Connaught Av. CO13: Frin S 5D 28
Connaught Cl. CO1: Colc 5E 14
    CO15: Clac S 7A 32
Connaught Gdns. E. CO15: Clac S 7A 32
Connaught Gdns. W. CO15: Clac S 7A 32
Connaught Ho. CO4: Colc 3E 6
Constable Av. CO16: Clac S 5E 30
Constable Cl. CO5: W Mer 4D 40
    CO11: Law 3D 10
Constable Ct. CO2: Colc 1H 21
Constable Rd. CO10: Sud 3E 36
Constantine Rd. CO3: Colc 6K 13
Constitution Hill CO10: Sud 3F 37
Conway Cl. CO7: W'hoe 4A 24
    CO9: Hals 5A 38
Cook Cl. CO12: Har 6E 26
Cook Cres. CO12: Har 4G 15
Cooks Cl. CO9: Hals 5C 38
Cooks Cres. CO7: W'hoe 5A 24
Cooks Hall Rd. CO6: W Ber 7C 4
Cook's La. CO3: Colc, S'way 3D 12
                        (not continuous)
Cooks Mill La. CO3: Ford H 1B 12
Cook's Shipyard CO7: W'hoe 4A 24
Coolyne Way CO15: Clac S 4A 32
Coopers Cres. CO6: W Ber 6F 5
Coopers La. CO15: Clac S 1F 35
Cooper Wlk. CO4: Colc 3F 15
Copford 2H 19
Copford Ct. CO6: M Tey 2G 19
COPFORD GREEN 4G 19
Copford St Michael & All Angels Church
    ....4K 19
Copperas Rd. CO7: B'sea 7H 41
Copper Beeches CO3: S'way 6D 12
Coppice, The CO15: Clac S 3G 35
Coppice End CO4: Colc 7D 6
Coppice Rd. CO7: Alr 4F 25
Coppingford End CO6: Cop 1H 19
Coppins Rd. CO15: Clac S 7F 31
Copse, The CO4: Colc 7B 6
Coralin Wlk. CO3: S'way 5C 12
Corinda Ho. CO13: Frin S 6D 28
Coriolanus Cl. CO2: Colc 1G 21
Cornard Rd. CO10: Sud 4F 37
CORNARD TYE 4K 37
Cornerth Cres. CO10: Gt Cor 5H 37
Cornflower Cl. CO3: S'way 4C 12
Cornflower Rd. CO15: Jay 5D 34
Cornford Way CO11: Law 3D 10

Cornwall Cl. CO11: Law 4D 10
Cornwallis Dr. CO6: M Tey 3C 18
Coronation Av. CO2: Colc 3C 22
Coronation Rd. CO15: Clac S 1F 35
Corporal Lillie Cl. CO10: Sud 5E 36
Corry Ct. CO4: Colc 3F 15
Cortoncroft Cl. CO13: Kir C 3D 28
Corunna Dr. CO2: Colc 2J 21
Cotman Av. CO11: Law 2D 10
Cotman Rd. CO3: Colc 6G 13
    CO16: Clac S 5G 31
Cotswold Cl. CO4: Colc 6E 6
Cotswold Rd. CO15: Clac S 6J 31
Cottage Dr. CO2: Colc 1E 22
Cottage Grn. CO16: Clac S 5F 31
Cottage Gro. CO16: Clac S 5F 31
Cottage Wlk. CO16: Clac S 5F 31
Cottonwood Cl. CO2: Colc 2K 21
Coulsdon Cl. CO16: Clac S 5F 31
County & Family Court
    Colchester 6A 42 (5A 14)
Courage Cl. CO4: Colc 4B 6
Courtauld Cl. CO9: Hals 4C 38
Courtauld Ct. CO2: Colc 4C 38
Courtauld Homes of Rest CO9: Hals ...2B 38
Courtenay Cl. CO10: Sud 1D 36
Courtlands CO9: Hals 5A 38
                        (off Abels Rd.)
Courtyards, The CO4: Colc 5E 6
Coventry Cl. CO1: Colc 3D 42 (3C 14)
Coverts, The CO5: W Mer 5D 40
Cowdray Av. CO1: Colc 1A 42 (2A 14)
Cowdray Cen., The CO1: Colc 1B 42 (2B 14)
Cowdray Cres. CO1: Colc 5C 42 (4B 14)
COWEY GREEN 3K 17
Cow La. CO7: Har 1K 27
Cowper Cres. CO4: Colc 7B 6
Cowslip Cl. CO3: S'way 4C 12
Cox Rd. CO7: Alr 4F 25
Cox's Ct. CO12: Har 2K 27
Cox's Hill CO11: Law 4C 10
Crabtree CO13: Kir S 2A 28
Crabtree La. CO6: L Hork 1C 4
Crabtree Cl. CO7: W'hoe 2K 23
Craig Ct. CO2: Colc 1H 21
                        (off Iceni Way)
Craigfield Av. CO15: Clac S 5J 31
Cranborne Cl. CO4: Colc 1B 14
Crane Av. CO3: S'way 7B 12
Cranford Cl. CO13: Frin S 5C 28
Cranleigh Cl. CO16: Clac S 5E 30
Cranmere Cl. CO1: Colc 4E 42 (4C 14)
Craven Dr. CO4: Colc 7E 6
Crayford Rd. CO10: Sud 1D 36
Credon Cl. CO15: Clac S 4J 31
Credon Dr. CO15: Clac S 4J 31
Creekhurst Cl. CO7: B'sea 6J 41
Creffield Rd. CO3: Colc 5K 13
Crescent, The CO4: Colc 4D 6
    CO6: Gt Hork 1H 5
    CO6: M Tey 3E 18
    CO6: W Ber 5E 4
    CO13: Frin S 5D 28
    CO15: Clac S 4A 32
Crescent Rd. CO14: Walt 2G 29
Crestlands CO7: Alr 5F 25
Cricketers Cl. CO10: Sud 5E 36
                        (off Priory Wlk.)
Crimea Wlk. CO2: Colc 7A 42 (6A 14)
Crispin Ct. CO1: Colc 4A 42 (4A 14)
CROCKLEFORD HEATH 1A 16
Crockleford Hill CO7: Crock H 2J 15
Crockleford Rd. CO7: Elm M 5D 16
Crocus Cl. CO16: Clac S 7F 31
Croft, The CO10: Sud 3E 36
Croft Cl. CO10: Sud 4E 36
Croft Rd. CO10: Sud 3E 36
    CO15: Clac S 7G 31
Crome Cl. CO3: Colc 6G 13
Cromer M. CO4: Colc 7A 6
Crome Rd. CO16: Clac S 5G 31
Cromwell Rd. CO2: Colc 7C 42 (5B 14)
Croquet Gdns. CO7: W'hoe 3A 24
Cross, The CO7: W'hoe 2K 23
Cross Cut Ct. CO1: Colc 5D 14
Crossfield Rd. CO15: Clac S 1H 35
Crossfield Way CO13: Kir C 4A 28
Cross La. CO5: W Mer 4E 40
Crossley Av. CO15: Jay 5B 34
Crossley Vw. CO15: Clac S 1K 35
Cross Rd. CO16: Clac S 6E 30
Cross St. CO10: Sud 4D 36
Crosstree Wlk. CO2: Colc 1C 22
Cross Way CO5: W Mer 4E 40

Crossways CO15: Jay 4D 34
Crouch St. CO3: Colc 6A 42 (5A 14)
(not continuous)
Crowhurst Ct. CO3: Colc 5A 42 (4A 14)
Crowhurst Rd. CO3: Colc 4A 14
Crown Bays Rd. CO4: Colc 3E 14
Crown Bus. Cen. CO7: A'lgh 3G 7
Crown Ct. CO4: Colc 4F 7
Crown Ga. CO4: Colc 4F 7
CROWN INTERCHANGE 3G 7
Crown La. CO12: Har 3J 27
Crown La. Nth. CO7: A'lgh 3G 7
Crown La. Sth. CO7: A'lgh 6J 7
Crown Rd. CO15: Clac S 3F 35
Crusader Bus. Pk. CO15: Clac S 3K 31
Crysrtal Wlk. CO2: Colc 7K 13
Cuckoo Farm Bus. Pk. CO4: Colc 3C 6
Cuckoo Farm Way CO4: Colc 3A 6
Culver Arc. CO1: Colc 5A 42 (4A 14)
Culver Shop. Cen. CO1: Colc 5A 42 (4A 14)
Culver Sq. CO1: Colc 5A 42
Culver St. E. CO1: Colc 5B 42 (4B 14)
Culver St. W. CO1: Colc 5A 42 (4A 14)
Culver Wlk. CO1: Colc 5B 42 (4B 14)
Cumberland Ct. CO15: Clac S 6A 32
Cunningham Cl. CO2: Colc 7C 14
(off Mulberry Av.)
Cunobelin Way CO2: Colc 2F 21
Curlew Cl. CO15: Clac S 5J 31
Curlew Cft. CO4: Colc 3H 15
Currents La. CO12: Har 1J 27
Curtis Cl. CO16: Clac S 1E 34
Curzon Rd. CO10: Sud 3H 37
Custom Ho. CO12: Har 3H 27
Custom Ho. La. CO12: Har 1J 27
Cut, The CO5: Tip 5G 39
Cutting Dr. CO9: Hals 4B 38
Cygnet Wlk. CO3: S'way 7B 12
Cymbeline Way CO3: Colc 4F 13
Cypress Cl. CO15: Clac S 4H 31
Cypress Gro. CO4: Colc 3G 15
Cypress M. CO5: W Mer 4B 40
Cyril Child Cl. CO4: Colc 4G 15

D

Dabchicks Sailing Club 4A 40
Dahlia Cl. CO16: Clac S 7F 31
Dahlia Wlk. CO4: Colc 4F 15
Daimler Av. CO15: Jay 5A 34
Dale, The CO7: W'hoe 4A 24
Dale Cl. CO3: S'way 4B 12
CO7: Elm M 5E 16
Dales, The CO12: Har 6E 26
Daltes La. CO16: St O 1A 34
Damask Rd. CO3: S'way 4C 12
Dame Mary Wlk. CO9: Hals 3D 38
Dammant Ct. CO4: Colc 3F 15
Danbury Cl. CO6: M Tey 3D 18
Danes Cl. CO10: Gt Cor 7H 37
Daniell Cl. CO15: Clac S 5F 31
Daniell Dr. CO2: Colc 2H 21
Daniells Ho. CO6: W Ber 6F 5
Dansie Ct. CO4: Colc 3E 14
Daphne Ct. CO4: Colc 3F 15
Dapifer Cl. CO2: Colc 7B 14
Darcy Cl. CO13: Kir C 4D 28
D'Arcy Hgts. CO2: Colc 1E 22
D'Arcy Rd. CO2: Colc 1E 22
CO5: Tip 7K 39
Darcy Way CO7: B'sea 5G 41
Darina Ct. CO3: S'way 4B 12
Darkhouse La. CO5: Rhdge 4J 23
Darnel Way CO3: S'way 4B 12
Darwin Cl. CO2: Colc 3D 22
Davall Cl. CO12: R'sy 6B 26
Davey Cl. CO1: Colc 5E 14
Davidson Cl. CO10: Gt Cor 7J 37
Davy Rd. CO15: Clac S 3B 32
Dawes La. CO5: W Mer 2E 40
Dawlish Rd. CO15: Clac S 4F 35
Dawnford Cl. CO3: S'way 4C 12
Dawnford Ct. CO3: S'way 4C 12
(off Dawnford Cl.)
Dead La. CO7: A'lgh 2A 8
CO11: Law, Mist 5D 10
CO13: Gt Hol 5A 28
CO16: L Cla, Wee H 4B 28
(not continuous)
Deal Cl. CO15: Clac S 4F 35
Deal Way CO7: B'sea 4G 41
Deanery Cl. CO10: Sud 1D 36
Deane's Cl. CO12: Har 5F 27

Deane's La. CO12: Har 6D 26
Deanhill Av. CO15: Clac S 6A 32
Dean St. CO7: B'sea 5G 41
Dean Wlk. CO4: Colc 5G 15
Deben Dr. CO10: Sud 3G 37
Deben Rd. CO4: Colc 2G 15
Deben Wlk. CO16: Clac S 5F 31
De Burgh Rd. CO3: Colc 5E 12
Dedham Av. CO16: Clac S 6E 30
Dedham Ct. CO2: Colc 7D 14
(off Stalin Rd.)
Dedham Rd. CO7: A'lgh 1B 8
CO11: Law 3A 10
Deepdale Rd. CO12: Har 3F 27
Defoe Cres. CO4: Colc 5K 5
De Grey Rd. CO4: Colc 3D 6
De Greys Cl. CO10: Gt Cor 6J 37
Delamere Rd. CO4: Colc 7F 7
Delius Wlk. CO4: Colc 4B 14
Dell, The CO1: Colc 6D 42 (4C 14)
CO10: Sud 5G 37
Denham Ct. CO7: W'hoe 4A 24
Denton's Ter. CO7: W'hoe 4K 23
Dereham Cl. CO2: Colc 1J 21
Derwent Gdns. CO15: Clac S 5B 32
Derwent Rd. CO4: Colc 5E 6
De Staunton Cl. CO7: Alr 5F 25
Devereaux Cl. CO14: Walt 2D 28
De Vere Ct. CO7: W'hoe 4K 23
De Vere La. CO7: W'hoe 3K 23
De Vere Rd. CO3: Colc 6G 13
De Veres Rd. CO9: Hals 4A 38
De Vere Way CO12: Har 5E 26
Devon Rd. CO2: Colc 1H 21
Devon Way CO12: Har 5C 26
CO15: Hol S 4D 32
Dewberry Cl. CO4: Colc 4F 15
Diamond Pl. CO3: Colc 5A 14
Diana Way CO15: Clac S 2G 35
Dickenson Rd. CO4: Colc 7A 6
Dickley Hall Chase CO11: Mist 7G 11
Digby M. CO5: W Mer 5C 40
Dilbridge Rd. E. CO4: Colc 3E 14
Dilbridge Rd. W. CO4: Colc 3D 14
Dinants Cres. CO6: M Tey 3C 18
Dinsdale Cl. CO4: Colc 3E 14
Distillery La. CO2: Colc 7E 14
Dixon Av. CO16: Clac S 5F 31
Dixon Cl. CO11: Law 3D 10
Dixon Way CO7: W'hoe 1J 23
(not continuous)
Dobbies La. CO6: M Tey 3D 18
Docker Ct. CO2: Colc 7D 14
(off Stalin Rd.)
Dockfield Av. CO12: Har 4E 26
Dodding's La. CO6: W'hoe 6C 18
Doggetts La. CO6: M Tey 4D 18
Dolphin Ct. CO13: Frin S 4F 29
Domitian Cl. CO4: Colc 5D 6
Domsey Bank CO6: M Tey 3C 18
Domsey Chase CO5: Fee 6A 18
Donard Dr. CO6: W Ber 6D 4
Donne Dr. CO15: Jay 4D 34
Donyland Way CO5: Rhdge 5H 23
Dooley Rd. CO9: Hals 4A 38
Dorchester End CO2: Colc 1D 22
Dorking Cres. CO16: Clac S 5F 31
Dorothy Curtice Ct. CO6: Cop 1J 19
Dorset Cl. CO9: Hals 4B 38
CO15: Hol S 5D 32
Douglas Rd. CO12: Har 4G 27
CO15: Clac S 7F 31
Dove Cres. CO12: Har 6C 26
Dovedale Gdns.
CO15: Clac S, Hol S 5B 32
Dove Ho. Mdw. CO10: Gt Cor 6G 37
Dover Cl. CO15: Clac S 4G 35
DOVERCOURT 4G 27
Dovercourt Bay Lifestyles 6G 27
Dovercourt Bowling Club 5H 27
Dovercourt By-Pass CO12: Har 3F 27
Dovercourt Haven Cvn. Pk.
CO12: Har 7F 27
Dovercourt Roller Skating Rink 5H 27
Dovercourt Station (Rail) 3J 27
Dover Rd. CO7: B'sea 4H 41
(not continuous)
Dowding Cl. CO2: Colc 7C 14
Downton Wlk. CO5: Tip 4H 39
Drake Rd. CO10: Sud 2G 37
Drakes App. CO15: Jay 3D 34
Dray Ct. CO6: W Ber 6F 5
Dresden Sq. CO16: Clac S 6E 30
Drift, The CO10: Gt Cor 5J 37

Drive, The CO12: Har 5G 27
CO15: Clac S 4A 32
Drury Dr. CO10: Sud 1F 37
Drury Rd. CO2: Colc 6J 13
Dry Dock CO7: W'hoe 4K 23
Dudley Cl. CO2: Colc 7C 14
Dudley Ct. CO15: Clac S 3K 31
Dudley Rd. CO15: Clac S 1G 35
Duffield Dr. CO4: Colc 4G 15
Dugard Av. CO3: Colc 7E 12
Dugmore Av. CO13: Kir S 2A 28
Duke St. CO7: B'sea 6G 41
Dulwich Rd. CO15: Hol S 7B 32
Duncan Rd. CO2: Colc 7H 13
Dunnock Way CO4: Colc 4H 15
Dunthorne Rd. CO4: Colc 1G 15
Dunthorpe Rd. CO16: Clac S 5G 31
Dunwich Ct. CO2: Colc 7B 14
Duoro M. CO2: Colc 2J 21
Dupont Cl. CO16: Clac S 5G 31
Durham Sq. CO1: Colc 4E 42 (4C 14)
DUTCH QUARTER 4A 42 (4A 14)
Dyer's Rd. CO3: S'way 1C 20

E

Eagle Av. CO14: Walt 1H 29
Eagle Dr. CO2: Colc 6C 14
Eaglegate CO1: Colc 4E 42 (4C 14)
Earlhams Cl. CO12: Har 6E 26
Earlhams M. CO12: Har 6C 26
Earls Hall Dr. CO16: Clac S 6B 30
Earlswood Lodge CO14: Walt 6J 29
Earlswood Way CO2: Colc 2K 21
East Bay CO1: Colc 4D 14
Eastcliff Av. CO15: Clac S 7A 32
E. Dock Rd. CO12: Har 1E 26
EAST END GREEN 6K 41
Easterling Cl. CO12: Har 3F 27
Eastern Rd. CO7: B'sea 6G 41
Easter Pk. CO4: Colc 3C 6
Eastgates CO1: Colc 4D 14
Eastgate St. CO12: Har 1J 27
East Haven CO15: Clac S 6H 31
East Hill CO1: Colc 4D 42 (4C 14)
EASTHORPE 6E 18
Easthorpe Grn. CO6: M Tey 5C 18
Easthorpe Rd. CO5: Ethpe 7A 18
CO6: Cop 6E 18
E. Mersea Rd. CO5: W Mer 1D 40
East Mill CO9: Hals 3C 38
Easton Way CO13: Frin S 4F 29
East Rd. CO5: W Mer 4D 40
E. Stockwell St. CO1: Colc 4B 42 (4B 14)
East St. CO1: Colc 4D 14
CO7: W'hoe 5K 23
CO10: Sud 4F 37
CO12: Har 3J 27
East Ter. CO14: Walt 1H 29
E. Ward M. CO1: Colc 4E 14
Eastwood Dr. CO4: Colc 6D 6
Eaton M. CO2: Colc 1D 22
Ebony Cl. CO2: Colc 2K 21
Edenside CO13: Kir C 3C 28
Edgefield Av. CO11: Law 4D 10
Edgware Rd. CO16: Clac S 6G 31
Edgworth Rd. CO10: Sud 4E 36
Edison Gdns. CO4: Colc 2E 14
Edison Rd. CO15: Hol S 5D 32
Edith Rd. CO13: Kir S 2B 28
CO15: Clac S 2H 35
Edward Av. CO7: B'sea 5H 41
Edward Paxman Gdns.
CO1: Colc 5E 14
Edwards Dr. CO7: Thorr 7K 25
Edward St. CO12: Har 2D 26
Egerton Grn. Rd. CO2: Colc 1G 21
Egremont Way CO3: S'way 7C 12
Egret Cres. CO4: A'lgh, Colc 3J 15
Eight Acre La. CO2: Colc 2J 21
EIGHT ASH GREEN 3A 12
EIGHT ASH GREEN INTERCHANGE
..............4B 12
Eld La. CO1: Colc 5B 42 (4B 14)
Eldon Cl. CO4: Colc 2G 15
Eldred Av. CO2: Colc 1H 21
Eldred Dr. CO10: Gt Cor 7J 37
Eleanor Cl. CO5: Tip 4H 39
Eleanor Wlk. CO5: Tip 4H 39
Electric Palace Cinema
Harwich 1K 27
(off Kings Quay St.)
Elfreda Ho. CO2: Colc 1H 21
(off Iceni Way)

Elianore Rd. CO3: Colc 4H 13
Elizabeth Cl. CO4: Colc 6E 6
Elizabeth Ct. CO10: Sud 3F 37
  CO12: Har .4F 27
  CO14: Walt .6J 29
Elizabeth Rd. CO12: Har 4F 27
Elizabeth Way CO7: B'sea 6H 41
  CO7: W'hoe 1A 24
  CO9: Hals .3B 38
  CO10: Ball .6C 36
Elliots Dr. CO14: Walt 2F 29
Ellis Rd. CO15: Clac S 2H 35
Elm Cl. CO5: Tip 3G 39
  CO7: Alr 4F 25
Elm Cres. CO4: Colc 4F 15
Elmcroft CO7: Elm M 5E 16
Elmdale Dr. CO11: Mann 4F 11
Elmden Ct. CO15: Clac S 6H 31
Elm Dr. CO7: B'sea 5F 41
  CO9: Hals .4C 38
  CO12: Har .4G 27
Elmfield Cl. CO15: Hol S 4D 32
Elm Gro. CO7: W'hoe 3K 23
  CO13: Kir C 4A 28
  CO15: Clac S 5J 31
  CO16: Clac S 2D 34
Elmhurst Rd. CO12: Har 4H 27
Elm Rd. CO10: Sud 4G 37
  CO16: L Cla 1F 31
ELMSTEAD 2E 16
ELMSTEAD HEATH 1E 24
ELMSTEAD MARKET 5E 16
Elmstead Rd. CO4: Colc 5F 15
  CO7: W'hoe, Elm M 1A 24
Elm Tree Av.
  CO13: Frin S, Walt 4D 28
  CO14: Walt .4D 28
Elm Tree Cl. CO13: Frin S 4D 28
Elmwood Av. CO2: Colc 2J 21
Elmwood Dr. CO5: W Mer 5D 40
Elstar La. CO6: Gt Hork 2H 5
Eltham Cl. CO2: Colc 7A 14
Elthorne Pk. CO15: Clac S 7G 31
Elton Wlk. CO5: Tip 4H 39
Elwes Cl. CO4: Colc 2F 15
Elwin Rd. CO5: Tip 5H 39
Ely Gdns.
  CO1: Colc 4E 42 (4C 14)
Emily May Ct. CO12: Har 4F 27
Empire Rd. CO12: Har 4J 27
Empire Theatre
  Halstead .3A 38
Empress Av. CO5: W Mer 4D 40
Empress Dr. CO5: W Mer 5D 40
Endean Ct. CO7: W'hoe 2J 23
Endeavour Way CO4: Colc 5B 6
Endsleigh Ct. CO3: Colc 4J 13
Engineers Sq. CO4: Colc 1K 13
Enid Way CO4: Colc 1K 13
Enoch Ho. CO4: Colc 3G 15
Enterprise Way CO15: Clac S 3A 32
Enville Way CO4: Colc 6D 6
Epping Cl. CO15: Clac S 3J 31
Epsom Cl. CO16: Clac S 5F 31
Erica Wlk. CO4: Colc 4F 15
Erle Havard Rd. CO6: W Ber 6E 4
Ernest Rd. CO7: W'hoe 3K 23
Ernulph Ct. CO1: Colc 5E 42 (4C 14)
Ernulph Wlk. CO1: Colc 5E 42 (4C 14)
Errington Rd. CO3: Colc 6K 13
Erskine Rd. CO11: Mann 3F 11
Esplanade CO15: Clac S 7D 28
Esplanade, The CO15: Hol S 5E 32
Essex Av. CO10: Sud 1F 37
  CO15: Jay .6B 34
ESSEX COUNTY HOSPITAL 5K 13
Essex Hall Rd. CO1: Colc 1A 42 (2A 14)
Essex St. CO2: Colc 6A 42 (5A 14)
Essex Yeomanry Way
  CO3: S'way 5B 12
Estella Ho. CO1: Colc 5A 42
Estuary Cl. CO4: Colc 6A 6
Estuary Cres. CO15: Clac S 1G 35
Estuary Pk. Rd. CO5: W Mer 5E 40
Eton Rd. CO13: Frin S 5E 28
  CO15: Clac S 7J 31
Eudo Ho. CO2: Colc 7B 14
Eudo Rd. CO2: Colc 7J 13
Europa Way CO12: Har 3E 26
Evans Ct. CO9: Hals 3C 38
Evergreen Dr. CO4: Colc 6F 7
Eves Ct. CO12: Har 6C 26
Ewan Cl. CO3: S'way 5C 12
Ewan Way CO3: S'way 5C 12
Ewer Cl. CO3: S'way 7D 12

Exeter Cl. CO6: Gt Hork 3H 5
Exeter Dr. CO1: Colc 4E 42 (4C 14)

F

Factory Hill CO5: Tip 6H 39
Factory La. CO11: Brant, Catt 1E 10
Factory La. E. CO9: Hals 3B 38
Factory La. W. CO9: Hals 4B 38
Factory Ter. CO9: Hals 3B 38
Fairbrother Cl. CO4: Colc 3F 15
Fair Cl. CO7: B'sea 6J 41
Fairclough Av. CO16: Clac S 1E 34
Fairfax Rd. CO2: Colc 7C 42 (5B 14)
Fairfax M. CO2: Colc 7C 42
Fairfield Gdns. CO4: Colc 3E 14
Fairfield Rd. CO15: Clac S 7H 31
Fairfield Way CO9: Hals 4C 38
Fairhaven Av. CO5: W Mer 4E 40
Fairhaven Ct. CO5: W Mer 6E 40
Fairhead Rd. Nth. CO4: Colc 3E 14
Fairhead Rd. Sth. CO4: Colc 3E 14
Fairlop Cl. CO15: Clac S 3J 31
Fairways CO4: Colc 7J 13
Falcon Cres. CO1: Colc 6D 14
Falcon Way CO15: Clac O 5J 31
Falcon Yd. CO7: W'hoe 4K 23
Falklands Dr. CO11: Mann 3F 11
Falklands Rd. CO2: Colc 1K 21
Fallowfield Cl. CO12: Har 4E 26
Fallowfield Rd. CO2: Colc 2J 21
Fan Av. CO4: Colc 1J 13
Fanny's La. CO16: Wee H 1A 30
Faraday Cl. CO15: Clac S 3K 31
Faraday Ho. CO2: Colc 7A 42 (6A 14)
Farford Fld. CO10: Gt Cor 5J 37
Farmers Way CO16: Clac S 1E 34
Farm Dr. CO6: Eig G 3A 12
Farmleigh Av. CO15: Clac S 3J 31
Farm Wlk. CO7: B'sea 4G 41
Farriers Chase CO5: W Mer 5D 40
Farriers End CO3: S'way 6D 12
Farthings Chase CO5: W Mer 5E 40
Faulds Wlk. CO2: Colc 1C 22
Feedhams Cl. CO7: W'hoe 1A 24
Felixstowe Cl. CO16: Clac S 7D 30
Fellowes Cl. CO4: Colc 1B 14
Felstead Cl. CO2: Colc 4C 22
Fen Chase CO7: Elm M 6C 16
Fen La. CO7: A'lgh 1B 8
Fennel Cl. CO5: Tip 5G 39
Fennings Chase CO1: Colc 5D 42 (4C 14)
Fenno Cl. CO3: Colc 7E 12
Fenn Rd. CO9: Hals 3D 38
Fenwick Dr. CO1: Colc 3D 14
Ferdinand Wlk. CO4: Colc 4H 15
Ferndale Rd. CO15: Clac S 4J 31
Ferndale Rd. CO12: Har 2J 27
Ferndown Rd. CO13: Frin S 5C 28
Fernlea Cl. CO4: Colc 1J 13
Fernlea Rd. CO12: Har 3J 27
Fern Way CO15: Jay 5C 34
Fernwood Av. CO15: Hol S 6E 32
Ferry Rd. CO5: Fing 6K 23
Fiat Av. CO15: Jay 6A 34
Field Cl. CO4: Colc 3G 15
Fieldgate Dock CO7: B'sea 7G 41
Fields Farm Rd. CO2: Lay H 7H 21
Fields Vw. CO10: Sud 3F 37
Field Vw. Cl. CO4: Colc 6B 6
Field Wlk. CO14: Walt 2E 28
Field Way CO7: W'hoe 2A 24
Fifth Av. CO9: Hals 4E 38
  CO13: Frin S 5C 28
Finchdale CO15: Clac S 5J 31
Finch Hill CO10: Bulm 4A 36
Finchingfield Way CO2: Colc 4C 22
Finch La. CO7: Elm M 6F 17
Finer Cl. CO16: Clac S 6F 31
FINGRINGHOE .7H 23
Fingringhoe Rd. CO2: Colc 2F 23
  CO5: Fing, Rhdge 4G 23
Finham Cl. CO4: Colc 4H 15
Finsbury Pl. CO9: Hals 3C 38
Firlie Wlk. CO2: Colc 2C 22
Firmins Ct. CO6: W Ber 6D 4
Firs, The CO2: Lay H 6G 21
Firs Cvn. Pk. CO16: L Cla 1G 31
Firs Chase CO5: W Mer 4A 40
Firs Chase Cvn. Pk. CO5: W Mer 4A 40
Firs Hamlet CO5: W Mer 5A 40
Firs Rd. CO5: Tip 6H 39
  CO5: W Mer 5B 40

First Av. CO9: Hals 4E 38
  CO10: Sud .2G 37
  CO12: Har .4H 27
  CO13: Frin S 6C 28
  CO14: Walt .6H 29
  CO15: Clac S 7A 32
Firstore Dr. CO3: Colc 4E 12
Firstsite Art Complex
  Colchester 5D 42 (4C 14)
Fir Tree Cl. CO4: Colc 6D 6
Fir Way CO15: Jay 6D 34
Firwood's Rd. CO9: Hals 5B 38
Fisin Wlk. CO3: Colc 1E 20
Fitzgerald Cl. CO11: Law 3D 10
Fitzgilbert Rd. CO2: Colc 7J 13
Fitzwalter Rd. CO3: Colc 5H 13
Fitzwilliam Rd. CO3: Colc 4H 13
Five Acres CO14: Walt 2F 29
Fivefields Cl. CO4: Colc 4G 15
Five Gables Chase CO5: W Mer 6D 40
Five Ways CO3: S'way 7D 12
Flagstaff Rd. CO2: Colc 7B 42 (5B 14)
Flail Cl. CO7: Elm M 5D 16
Flame Way CO4: Colc 4B 6
Flanders Fld. CO2: Colc 1D 22
Flatford Dr. CO16: Clac S 7E 30
Flatford Mill 1A 10
Flavius Way CO4: Colc 4C 6
Fleece Yd. CO9: Hals 3B 38
Fleetwood Av. CO15: Hol S 4C 32
Fleetwood Cl. CO15: Hol S 4D 32
Fleming Ho. CO2: Colc 7A 42 (6A 14)
Flemish Cl. CO1: Colc 3B 42
Flixton Cl. CO16: Clac S 7D 30
Flood La. CO4: Colc 4E 6
Florence Rd. CO14: Walt 7H 29
Flowers Way CO15: Jay 5D 34
Folkards La. CO7: B'sea 4H 41
Folley, The CO2: Lay H 6G 21
  CO3: S'way 6D 12
Folly, The CO5: Tip 7K 39
  CO7: W'hoe 5K 23
Fordham Rd. CO6: W Ber 2B 4
Ford La. CO7: Alr, B'sea 7E 24
Ford Rd. CO15: Clac S 1G 35
Ford Rd. Ind. Est. CO15: Clac S 1G 35
Fords La. CO4: Colc 6J 5
Fordwich Rd. CO7: B'sea 3G 41
Foresight Rd. CO2: Colc 2F 23
Forester's Ct. CO7: W'hoe 3K 23
Forest Pk. Av. CO15: Clac S 4H 31
Forest Rd. CO4: Colc 4F 15
Forge Ct. CO7: A'lgh 3C 8
Forres CO13: Frin S 6D 28
Fortius M. CO4: Colc 5B 6
Fossetts La. CO6: For 5A 4
Foster Rd. CO12: Har 2D 26
Foundation Way CO2: Colc 3A 22
Foundry Cl. CO11: Law 3E 10
Foundry La. CO6: Cop 1H 19
                 (not continuous)
Fountain Ct. CO5: W Mer 4D 40
Fountain La. CO3: Heck 6J 19
  CO6: Cop, Heck 6J 19
Fourth Av. CO9: Hals 4E 38
  CO13: Frin S 5D 28
  CO15: Clac S 7B 32
Fowler Rd. CO2: Colc 3A 22
FOXASH ESTATE 1G 9
Foxendale Cl. CO3: S'way 4C 12
Foxglove Cl. CO15: Clac S 4J 31
Foxglove Wlk. CO4: Colc 4G 15
FOX STREET 6J 7
Frances Cl. CO7: W'hoe 2K 23
Francis Cl. CO5: Tip 6G 39
Francis Ct. CO6: M Tey 2G 19
Francis Kellerman Wlk. CO3: Colc 4A 14
Francis Rd. CO10: Sud 4E 36
Francis St. CO7: B'sea 7H 41
Francis Way CO4: Colc 2F 15
Frank Clater Cl. CO4: Colc 3E 14
Frank Naylor Ct. CO1: Colc 4B 42
FRATING 3J 25
FRATING GREEN 1K 25
Frating Hill CO7: Frat, Elm M 1H 25
Frating Pk. CO7: Frat 1K 25
Frating Rd. CO7: A'lgh 4D 8
  CO7: Frat, Gt Bro 5K 17
  CO7: Thorr .4K 25
Freeland Rd. CO15: Clac S 3H 35
Freelands CO7: B'sea 6K 41
Freeman Cl. CO4: Colc 4C 6
Free Rodwell Ho. CO11: Mist 3H 11
              (off Barley Cl.)
Fremantle Rd. CO2: Colc 3D 22

Frensham Cl. CO3: S'way 4D 12
Frere Way CO5: Fing 6K 23
Freshfields CO12: Har 6E 26
Freshfields Rd. CO12: Har 3F 27
Freshwater La. CO15: Clac S 3J 31
Friars Cl. CO4: Colc 1E 14
CO7: W'hoe 4A 24
CO15: Clac S 5H 31
Friars Ct. CO2: Colc 1E 22
Friars St. CO10: Sud 4E 36
Friday Wood Grn. CO2: Colc 4B 22
Frietuna Rd. CO13: Kir C 4C 28
Frinton & Walton Swimming Pool 1H 29
Frinton Cl. CO13: Frin S 7D 28
Frinton Golf Course 1K 33
FRINTON-ON-SEA 6D 28
Frinton-on-Sea Station (Rail) 5D 28
Frinton Rd. CO13: Kir C 4A 28
CO15: Hol S 6C 32
Frobisher Dr. CO15: Jay 3C 34
Frobisher Rd. CO12: Har 6E 26
Frog Hall Cl. CO5: Fing 6A 24
Fronk's Av. CO12: Har 5H 27
Fronk's Rd. CO12: Har 4F 27
Frowick La. CO16: St O, Wee H 1A 30
Fryatt Av. CO12: Har 3F 27
FRYATT HOSPITAL
(& MAYFLOWER MEDICAL CENTRE) ...4F 27
Fuchsia Cl. CO4: Colc 3F 15
Fuchsia Way CO16: Clac S 6F 31
Fuller's Rd. CO2: Colc 2F 23
Fulmar Cl. CO4: Colc 3J 15
Fulmar Ho. CO12: Har 3H 27
Furneaux La. CO5: Fing 7H 23
Furrow Cl. CO3: S'way 6E 12
Furze Cres. CO7: Alr 5E 24

G

Gables, The CO12: Har 4J 27
Gager Dr. CO5: Tip 5J 39
Gainsborough Cl. CO5: W Mer 5D 40
CO16: Clac S 5E 30
Gainsborough Dr. CO11: Law 3D 10
Gainsborough Rd. CO3: Colc 6G 13
CO10: Sud 3E 36
Gainsborough's House 4E 36
Gainsborough St. CO10: Sud 4E 36
Gainsford Av. CO15: Clac S 7A 32
Gala Bingo
Clacton-on-Sea 1H 35
Colchester 6C 42
Gala Cl. CO6: Gt Hork 3H 5
Galloway Dr. CO16: L Cla 1F 31
Game Cl. CO10: Gt Cor 7H 37
Gantry Cl. CO1: Colc 5D 14
Gaol La. CO10: Sud 4E 36
Gap, The CO15: Hol S 5F 33
Garden Ct. CO13: Frin S 7D 28
Garden Dr. CO3: Colc 5E 12
Gardeners Rd. CO9: Hals 4C 38
Garden Farm CO5: W Mer 4D 40
Gardenia Pl. CO16: Clac S 7E 30
Gardenia Wlk. CO4: Colc 4G 15
Garden Pl. CO10: Sud 4D 36
Garden Rd. CO14: Walt 3E 28
CO15: Jay 5D 34
Garden Ter. CO9: Hals 3C 38
Garland Rd. CO2: Colc 7A 42 (6A 14)
CO12: Har 2E 26
Garlands Rd. CO2: B'ch, Lay H 7D 20
Garling Wlk. CO6: W Ber 7E 4
Garret Pl. CO6: W Ber 6F 5
Garrison Pde. CO2: Colc 7D 42 (6C 14)
Garrod Ct. CO2: Colc 5D 22
Garthwood Cl. CO6: W Ber 6E 4
Gascoigne Rd. CO4: Colc 3E 14
Gasfield CO11: Mann 3F 11
(off Malthouse Rd.)
Gatacre Ct. CO2: Colc 1H 21
Gatefield Cl. CO14: Walt 3D 28
Gate Ho. M. CO5: Tip 6H 39
Gavin Way CO4: Colc 5C 6
Gazelle Ct. CO4: Colc 6D 6
Gentian Cl. CO4: Colc 1J 33
Geoff Seaden Cl. CO1: Colc 5E 14
George Av. CO4: Colc 5H 41
George CO15: Clac S 2F 35
George Cut CO7: B'sea 4H 41
George St. CO1: Colc 4B 42 (4B 14)
CO12: Har 1J 27
George Williams Way CO1: Colc ..6E 42 (5C 14)
Geranium Cl. CO16: Clac S 7F 31
Geranium Wlk. CO4: Colc 4F 15

Gerard Rd. CO16: Clac S 5F 31
Gernon Rd. CO7: A'lgh 3C 8
Gilberd Cl. CO4: Colc 4E 6
Gilberd Ho. CO3: Colc 4G 13
Gilberd Rd. CO2: Colc 6D 14
Gilbert Ct. CO1: Colc 1A 42 (2A 14)
Gilderdale Cl. CO4: Colc 7F 7
Gilders Way CO16: Clac S 6F 31
Gilwell Pk. Cl. CO3: Colc 7G 13
Gipsy La. CO12: Har 6C 26
Girling St. CO10: Sud 3E 36
Glade, The CO4: Colc 1G 15
Gladeview CO15: Clac S 4J 31
Gladiator Way CO2: Colc 2F 21
Gladstone Rd. CO1: Colc 7E 42 (6D 14)
CO5: Tip 6H 39
Gladwin Rd. CO2: Colc 7J 13
Glebe Cl. CO7: Elm M 5E 16
Glebelands CO6: Gt Hork 1H 5
Glebe Rd. CO2: Colc 2J 21
CO5: Tip 5G 39
Glebe Vw. CO5: W Mer 4E 40
Glebe Way CO13: Frin S 5D 28
CO15: Jay 5D 34
Glen Av. CO3: Colc 4H 13
Glendale Gro. CO4: Colc 7E 6
Glenside CO10: Gt Cor 5G 37
Glentress Ct. CO4: Colc 7F 7
Glenway Cl. CO6: Gt Hork 1H 5
Glisson Sq. CO2: Colc 7H 13
Globe Cl. CO5: Tip 4H 39
Globe Wlk. CO5: Tip 4H 39
Globe Yd. CO10: Sud 3E 36
(off Inkerman Row)
Gloucester Av. CO2: Colc 1J 21
Gloucester Way CO10: Sud 1D 36
Glover Cl. CO16: Clac S 5E 30
Gnome Magic 1J 7
Go Bananas
Colchester 1B 42 (2B 14)
Godmans La. CO6: M Tey 3B 18
Godwin Cl. CO9: Hals 4A 38
Goings La. CO5: W Mer 5D 40
Goldcrest Cl. CO4: A'lgh, Colc 3H 15
Golden Dawn Way CO4: Colc 1A 14
Golden Lion La. CO12: Har 2K 27
Golden Noble Hill CO1: Colc 7D 42 (5C 14)
Goldfinch Cl. CO4: Colc 4H 15
Golf Grn. Rd. CO15: Jay 4D 34
Goodey Cl. CO1: Colc 7E 42 (6C 14)
Goodlake CO12: Har 5E 26
Goojerat Rd. CO2: Colc 6K 13
Gordian Wlk. CO4: Colc 4D 6
Gordon Dr. CO4: Colc 5E 6
Gordon Rd. CO12: Har 5G 27
Gordon Way CO12: Har 5G 27
Goring Rd. CO4: Colc 2E 14
Gorse La. CO5: Tip 6H 39
CO15: Clac S 3K 31
Gorse La. Ind. Est. CO15: Clac S 3A 32
Gorse Wlk. CO4: Colc 4H 15
(not continuous)
Gorse Way CO3: S'way 7D 12
CO15: Jay 5C 34
Gosbecks Rd. CO2: Colc 1G 21
Gosbeck's Vw. CO2: Colc 2G 21
Gosfield Rd. CO2: Colc 4C 22
Goslings Av. CO14: Walt 2F 29
Gosfield Rd. CO14: Walt 3E 28
Graces Wlk. CO13: Frin S 4E 28
Grafton Rd. CO12: Har 3J 27
Grammar School Pl. CO10: Sud 4E 36
Granchester Ct. CO4: Colc 6E 6
(off Bignell Cft.)
Grand, The CO15: Clac S 2K 35
Grange Cl. CO9: Hals 6B 38
CO14: Walt 3E 28
Grange Farm Pk. CO2: Colc 7F 15
Grange Farm Rd. CO2: Colc 7F 15
Grange Rd. CO5: Tip 4F 39
CO6: Gt Hork 3H 5
CO11: Law, L Bro 4H 9
CO12: Har 5F 27
Grange Way CO2: Colc 7F 15
Grange Way Bus. Pk. CO2: Colc 1F 23
Grantham Av. CO10: Gt Cor 1H 37
Grantham Cl. CO1: Colc 4D 42 (4C 14)
Grantham Rd. CO6: Gt Hork 3H 5
Grantley Cl. CO4: Colc 1H 19
Granville Cl. CO6: W Ber 4H 5
Granville Rd. CO1: Colc 6D 14
CO15: Clac S 1J 35
Granville Way CO7: B'sea 5J 41
Grasby Cl. CO7: W'hoe 2K 23
Grasmere Gdns. CO13: Kir C 3D 28

Grassfields CO13: Kir C 4C 28
Grassmere CO4: Colc 5D 6
Grass Rd. CO9: Hals 7A 38
Gratian Cl. CO4: Colc 5D 6
Gravel Hill Way CO12: Har 6D 26
Grayling Dr. CO4: Colc 2H 15
Gray Rd. CO3: Colc 5K 13
Grays Cl. CO5: W Mer 5C 40
Grays Cotts. CO1: Colc 4D 14
Gt. Bentley Rd. CO7: Frat, Thorr 1K 25
GREAT BROMLEY 2J 17
GREAT CLACTON 6J 31
GREAT CORNARD 6H 37
Great Cornard Country Pk. 7J 37
Great Cornard Sports Cen. 7H 37
Gt. Eastern Ct. CO14: Walt 3G 29
Gt. Eastern Rd. CO10: Sud 4F 37
Greate Ho. Farm Rd. CO2: Lay H 7G 21
Great Harrods CO14: Walt 3E 28
GREAT HOLLAND COMMON 1C 32
Gt. Holland Comn. Rd. CO15: Clac S 1C 32
Great Holland Pits Nature Reserve 1D 32
GREAT HORKESLEY 2H 5
Gt. Tey Rd. CO6: Gt Tey, L Tey 1A 18
Great Yd. CO9: Hals 5B 38
Green, The CO11: Mist 3H 11
CO12: Har 5D 26
CO16: Clac S 2E 34
Greenacres CO4: Colc 7A 6
CO15: Clac S 6K 31
Greenacres Cvn. Pk. CO12: Har 6F 27
Green Acres Rd. CO2: Lay H 7F 21
Greenbanks CO9: Hals 4A 38
Greenfields CO13: Kir C 3D 28
Greenfinch End CO4: Colc 3H 15
Greenford Rd. CO15: Clac S 1F 35
Greenhurst Rd. CO7: B'sea 6J 41
Green Island Gdns. 7D 8
Green La. CO4: Colc 7G 7
CO5: Tip 4H 39
CO6: Gt Hork 4J 5
CO7: A'lgh 3B 8
CO7: Crock H 2K 15
CO11: Mist 4F 11
CO14: Walt 7H 29
Greenlawns CO16: L Cla 1F 31
Greensmill CO11: Law 2D 10
GREENSTEAD 5G 15
Greenstead Ct. CO1: Colc 5F 15
CO2: Colc 4E 14
Greenstead Rd. CO1: Colc 4E 14
CO2: Colc 4E 14
GREENSTEAD GREEN 7D 38
GREENSTEAD RDBT. 5F 15
Green's Yd. CO1: Colc 4A 42 (4A 14)
Greenview CO14: Walt 1H 29
Greenview Pk. CO15: Clac S 5K 31
Greenway CO13: Frin S 5D 28
Greenway, The CO15: Clac S 4A 32
Greenway Cl. CO15: Clac S 4A 32
Greenwood CO9: Hals 3C 38
Greenwood Gro. CO4: Colc 7E 6
Gregory St. CO10: Sud 4E 36
Grendel Way CO15: Hol S 5E 32
Grenfell Av. CO15: Hol S 4D 32
Grenfell Cl. CO4: Colc 2E 14
Grenville Rd. CO10: Sud 1F 37
Gresley Cl. CO4: Colc 1B 14
Greville Cl. CO14: Walt 7J 29
Greyfriars Ct. CO1: Colc 4C 42 (4B 14)
Greystones CO3: Colc 1G 21
Grier Way CO16: Clac S 5E 30
Grieves Ct. CO3: S'way 7C 12
Grigson Dr. CO16: Clac S 6D 30
Grimston Rd. CO2: Colc 7C 14
Grimston Way CO14: Walt 3F 29
Groome Ct. CO4: Colc 4F 15
Groom Ho. CO15: Clac S 7H 31
Groom Pk. CO15: Clac S 7H 31
Grosvenor Cl. CO5: Tip 5H 39
Grosvenor Pl. CO5: Tip 4D 14
Grosvenor Rd. CO10: Sud 1D 36
Grove, The CO15: Clac S 2J 35
Grove Av. CO5: W Mer 6C 40
CO14: Walt 2F 29
Grove Cotts. CO6: Cop 4H 19
Grove Flats, The CO14: Walt 2F 29
Grove Rd. CO5: Tip 5H 39
Groves Cl. CO4: Colc 1A 14
Grymes Dyke Ct. CO3: S'way 5E 12
Gryme's Dyke Way CO3: S'way 1E 20
Gryphon Rd. CO2: Colc 7A 14
Gryps Cl. CO2: Colc 4E 14
Guildford Rd. CO1: Colc 2D 42 (3C 14)
Gunfleet Cl. CO5: W Mer 4B 40
Gunfleet Ct. CO15: Clac S 7B 32

Gunner M. CO1: Colc 5D 14
(off Cannon St.)
Gurdon Rd. CO2: Colc 1B 22
Gurney Benham Cl. CO2: Colc 7H 13
Guy Cook Cl. CO10: Gt Cor 6J 37
Gwynne Rd. CO12: Har 3J 27
Gypsy La. CO5: Ethpe 7A 18
CO10: Ball 4B 36

H

Haddon Pk. CO1: Colc 5E 14
Hadleigh Ct. CO15: Clac S 1K 35
Hadleigh Rd. CO13: Frin S 5D 28
CO16: Clac S 7E 30
Hadrian Cl. CO4: Colc 4D 6
Haggars La. CO7: Frat 1K 25
Hakewill Way CO4: Colc 7A 6
Hale Way CO4: Colc 4D 6
Halfacre La. CO12: Har 5F 27
Hall Barn CO5: W Mer 5B 40
Hall Chase CO6: M Tey 3F 19
Hall Cottages, The CO6: Cop 4J 19
Hall Cres. CO15: Hol S 5E 32
Hallcroft Chase CO4: Colc 6E 6
Hall Cut CO7: B'sea 6H 41
Hall Lo. CO7: Thorn 1K 41
CO12: Har 5F 27
CO14: Walt 7H 29
Hall Ri. CO10: Ball 6C 36
Hall Rd. CO5: Tip 6G 39
CO6: Cop 3J 19
CO6: W Ber 5C 4
CO7: Gt Bro 7F 9
CO10: Borl 1A 36
Hall Rd. Cotts. CO6: W Ber 4D 4
HALSTEAD 3B 38
Halstead Heritage Mus. 4B 38
HALSTEAD HOSPITAL 2B 38
Halstead Leisure Cen. 3D 38
Halstead Rd. CO3: Colc, S'way 4B 12
CO6: Aldh, Eig G 3A 12
CO9: G'std G 7D 38
CO13: Kir C, Kir S 4A 28
Hamford Cl. CO14: Walt 6H 29
Hamilton Rd. CO3: Colc 6K 13
CO7: W'hoe 4K 23
CO10: Sud 4E 36
Hamilton St. CO12: Har 2E 26
Hamlet Dr. CO4: Colc 4H 15
Hammond Ct. CO13: Frin S 5D 28
Hampstead Av. CO16: Clac S 6F 31
Hampton Ct. Cl. CO2: Colc 7K 13
Hanbury Gdns. CO4: Colc 5D 6
Handel Wlk. CO4: Colc 5G 15
Handford Pl. CO3: Colc 5K 13
Handy Fisher Ct. CO3: Colc 7H 13
Hangings, The CO12: Har 3G 27
Hankin Av. CO12: Har 6B 26
Hanningfield Way CO4: Colc 5D 6
Hanover Ct. CO10: Sud 5D 36
CO12: Har 4H 27
CO14: Walt 2E 28
Hanwell Cl. CO16: Clac S 6G 31
Harborough Hall La. CO5: Mess 1J 39
Harbour Cres. CO12: Har 2K 27
Harbour Sq. CO7: B'sea 7G 41
Harcourt Av. CO12: Har 3F 27
Hardies Point CO2: Colc 6F 15
Hardings Yd. CO7: W'hoe 5K 23
(off The Quay)
Hardy Ct. CO10: Sud 1F 37
HARDY'S GREEN 7J 19
Harebell Cl. CO4: Colc 7D 6
Hares Wlk. CO10: Sud 3F 37
Hargood Cl. CO3: Colc 4E 12
Harman Wlk. CO16: Clac S 6F 31
Harold Cl. CO9: Hals 4C 38
Harold Collins Pl. CO1: Colc 4D 14
Harold Gro. CO13: Frin S 6D 28
Harold Rd. CO13: Frin S 6D 28
CO15: Clac S 1J 35
Harold Way CO13: Frin S 6D 28
Harp Cl. Rd. CO10: Sud 3F 37
Harpers Way CO16: Clac S 1D 34
Harp Mdw. La. CO2: Colc 7K 13
Harrington Cl. CO5: Tip 5F 39
Harrison Ct. CO5: W Mer 5C 40
Harrison Rd. CO2: Colc 1B 22
Harrow Rd. CO15: Clac S 7J 31
Harsnett Rd. CO1: Colc 6D 14
Hartest Way CO10: Gt Cor 5H 37
Hart's La. CO7: A'lgh 1H 7
Harvard Ct. CO4: Colc 6D 6

Harvest Cl. CO6: M Tey 2F 19
Harvest Ct. CO6: Gt Hork 1H 5
Harvest End CO3: S'way 6D 12
Harvest Way CO7: Elm M 5D 16
Harvey Cl. CO11: Law 3D 10
Harvey Cres. CO3: S'way 7C 12
Harvey Rd. CO2: Colc 2H 21
CO7: W'hoe 3K 23
Harvey St. CO9: Hals 3C 38
HARWICH 3J 27
Harwich & Dovercourt Golf Course 3E 26
Harwich Gateway Retail Pk. CO12: Har ...3E 26
Harwich Gro. CO4: Colc 4E 14
Harwich Ind. Est. CO12: Har 2E 26
Harwich International Port 1D 26
Harwich International Station (Rail) 1E 26
Harwich Lifeboat Mus. 1K 27
Harwich Lifeboat Station 1K 27
Harwich Redoubt 2K 27
Harwich Rd. CO4: Colc 4E 14
CO7: A'lgh 6K 7
CO7: A'lgh, Law 2D 8
CO7: Gt Bro 5H 17
CO11: Law 5A 10
CO11: Mist 3J 11
CO12: L Oak 7B 26
Harwich Sports Cen. 0F 27
Harwich Town Station (Rail) 2J 27
Harwich Treadwheel Crane, The (Re-erected)
....1K 27
Harwood Cl. CO2: Colc 7C 14
Haslemere Gdns. CO13: Kir C 3D 28
Hastings Av. CO15: Clac S 4F 35
Hastings Pl. CO7: B'sea 4H 41
Hastings Rd. CO3: Colc 7G 13
Hatchcroft Gdns. CO7: Elm M 5E 16
Hatcher Cres. CO2: Colc 6E 14
Haubourdin Ct. CO9: Hals 3D 38
Haven, The CO12: Har 4E 26
Haven Av. CO15: Hol S 5F 33
Havencroft Ct. CO14: Walt 2G 29
Haven Rd. CO2: Colc 6F 15
Havenvale Ct. CO15: Clac S 7H 31
Haven Village 6G 41
Havering Cl. CO4: Colc 2D 14
CO15: Clac S 4H 31
Hawfinch Rd. CO2: Lay H 7G 21
Hawkendon Rd. CO16: Clac S 7D 30
Hawkesway CO15: Clac S 5J 31
Hawkins Cl. CO10: Sud 1F 37
Hawkins Rd. CO2: Colc 5F 15
CO7: Alr 4F 25
CO10: Sud 1G 37
Hawlmark End CO6: M Tey 3C 18
Hawthorn Av. CO4: Colc 3G 15
CO9: Hals 2D 38
Hawthorn Cl. CO9: Hals 2D 38
CO15: Clac S 4H 31
Hawthorns CO13: Kir C 3D 28
Hawthorns, The CO10: Sud 1G 37
Haye La. CO5: Fing 7E 22
Hayes Grn. Rd. CO5: Lay M 1K 39
Hayes Rd. CO15: Clac S 2H 35
Hayward Ct. CO1: Colc 4E 14
Hazell Av. CO2: Colc 1G 21
Hazell Ct. CO10: Sud 3F 37
(off Acton La.)
Hazel M. CO7: B'sea 5G 41
Hazelton Rd. CO4: Colc 2F 15
Hazelville Cl. CO12: Har 6D 26
Hazelwood Cres. CO16: L Cla 2F 31
Hazlemere Rd. CO15: Hol S 7B 32
Headgate CO3: Colc 6A 42 (5A 14)
Headgate Bldg. CO1: Colc 6A 42
(off Sir Isaac's Wlk.)
Headgate Ct. CO1: Colc 5A 42
Headgate Theatre, The 6A 42
Head La. CO10: Gt Cor 7G 37
Head St. CO1: Colc 5A 42 (4A 14)
CO5: Rhdge 4J 23
CO9: Hals 3C 38
Head Way CO10: Sud 1D 36
Heath, The CO2: Lay H 6G 21
Heath Bus. Pk. CO2: Colc 1F 23
Heather Cl. CO2: Lay H 7F 21
CO15: Clac S 4A 32
Heather Dr. CO3: Colc 6F 13
Heathfields CO6: Eig G 3A 12
Heathfields Ho. CO2: Colc 1E 22
Heath Rd. CO3: Colc 6F 13
CO3: Ford H 4J 9
CO3: S'way 7D 12
CO5: Rhdge 4H 23
CO7: Alr 4F 25

Heath Rd. CO7: W'hoe 2K 23
CO11: Mist 5K 11
CO16: St O, Wee H 2A 30
Heathside CO6: W Ber 6E 4
Heathview CO11: Mist 4K 11
Heatley Way CO4: Colc 3H 15
Heaton Way CO5: Tip 4H 39
HECKFORDBRIDGE 4A 20
Heckworth Cl. CO4: Colc 4E 6
Hedge Dr. CO2: Colc 1H 21
Hedgelands CO6: Cop 1H 19
Hedgerows CO3: S'way 5D 12
Hedingham Rd. CO9: Hals 1A 38
Heia Wharf CO2: Colc 5F 15
Helen Ewing Pl. CO2: Colc 3B 22
Helm Cl. CO6: Gt Hork 3J 5
Hendon Cl. CO16: Clac S 6G 31
Henley Ct. CO3: Colc 5F 13
Henrietta Cl. CO7: W'hoe 1A 24
Henry Cl. CO15: Clac S 2F 35
Henry Everett Gro. CO2: Colc 3B 22
Henry Laver Ct. CO3: Colc 4A 14
Henry Swan Way CO1: Colc 2C 42 (3B 14)
Henry Villa Cl. CO4: Colc 6K 5
Herbert Cl. CO10: Sud 1G 37
Herbert Rd. CO15: Clac S 1H 35
Hereford Cl. CO15: Hol S 6D 32
Hereford Rd. CO1: Colc 4E 42 (4C 14)
CO15: Hol S 6D 32
Hereward Cl. CO7: W'hoe 1A 24
Heron Cl. CO3: S'way 7B 12
Heron Glade CO15: Clac S 4J 31
Heronsgate CO13: Frin S 4D 28
Heron Way CO12: Har 3H 27
CO13: Kir C 4C 28
Herrick Pl. CO3: Colc 5G 13
Hervilly Way CO14: Walt 3F 29
Heseltine Ct. CO15: Clac S 7A 32
Hesper Rd. CO2: Colc 6E 14
Hetherington Ct. CO2: Colc 4C 22
Hewes Cl. CO4: Colc 4H 15
Hewitt Rd. CO12: Har, R'sy 6B 26
Heybridge Ct. CO15: Clac S 7A 32
(off Connaught Gdns. E.)
Heycroft Way CO5: Tip 4H 39
Hickory Av. CO4: Colc 3F 15
Highbirch Rd. CO16: Wee H 1A 30
Highbury Ter. CO9: Hals 3C 38
Highbury Vw. CO10: Gt Cor 5H 37
Highclere Rd. CO4: Colc 6D 6
Highfield Av. CO12: Har 4G 27
Highfield Dr. CO3: Colc 5J 13
Highfield Holiday Pk. CO16: Clac S 3H 31
Highfield Rd. CO10: Sud 2G 37
Highfields CO9: Hals 5B 38
Highlands Dr. CO15: Clac S 4J 31
Highlands Gro. CO15: Clac S 4K 31
High Lighthouse
Harwich 2K 27
High Oaks CO12: Har 5A 26
HIGH PARK CORNER 6K 23
High Rd. CO2: Lay H 7F 21
High St. CO1: Colc 5A 42 (4A 14)
CO5: Rhdge 4J 23
CO5: W Mer 5B 40
CO7: B'sea 6H 41
CO7: W'hoe 4K 23
CO9: Hals 3B 38
CO11: Mann, Mist 3F 11
CO11: Mist 3H 11
CO12: Har 3J 27
CO14: Walt 2G 29
CO15: Clac S 2J 35
High St. Nth. CO5: W Mer 5C 40
High Tree La. CO14: Walt 7H 29
High Vw. Av. CO15: Clac S 5H 31
High Vw. Cl. CO15: Clac S 5H 31
Highview Cl. CO10: Sud 1E 36
HIGHWOODS 6D 6
Highwoods App. CO4: Colc 6D 6
High Woods Country Pk. 7C 6
High Woods Country Pk. Vis. Cen. 7B 6
Highwoods Sq. CO4: Colc 6D 6
Hillcrest CO13: Kir S 2B 28
CO15: Clac S 5K 31
Hillcrest Ct. CO12: Har 4H 27
Hillcrest Rd. CO10: Sud 1E 36
Hill Ho. Ct. CO7: B'sea 5J 41
Hillman Av. CO15: Jay 6B 34
Hillridge CO4: Colc 7D 6
Hill Rd. CO12: Har 3H 27
CO15: Clac S 5H 31
Hills Cres. CO3: Colc 6G 13
Hillside CO13: Frin S 6C 28
Hillside Cres. CO15: Hol S 5B 32

Hillside Rd. CO10: Sud 4G 37
Hillsleigh M. CO1: Colc 5E 42 (4C 14)
Hillston Cl. CO2: Colc 2D 22
Hilltop Cl. CO2: Colc 7F 15
Hillview Cl. CO5: Rhdge 4H 23
Hillybroom Gdns. CO5: W Mer 5D 40
Hilton Cl. CO11: Mann 3F 11
Hitchcock Pl. CO10: Sud 2E 36
Hobart Gdns. CO2: Colc 2C 22
Hoe Dr. CO3: Colc 6G 13
Hogarth Cl. CO5: W Mer 5D 40
Hogarth End CO13: Kir C 3C 28
Holborough Cl. CO4: Colc 4H 15
Holbrook Cl. CO16: Clac S 7E 30
Holbrooke Wlk. CO5: Tip 5J 39
                    (off Wilkin Dr.)
Holden Rd. CO4: Colc 1B 14
Holland Haven Country Pk. 3G 33
HOLLAND-ON-SEA 5C 32
Holland Pk. CO15: Clac S 7K 31
Holland Rd. CO13: Frin S 7C 28
      CO13: Kir C 4A 28
      CO15: Clac S 2J 35
                      (Church Rd.)
      CO15: Clac S 1K 35
                       (Vista Rd.)
      CO16: Clac S, L Cla 1G 31
Holledge Cres. CO13: Kir C 4C 28
Holliwell Cl. CO3: S'way 5D 12
Holly Cl. CO2: Colc 2J 21
      CO12: Har 3J 27
Holly Ct. CO15: Clac S 7H 31
Hollymead Cl. CO4: Colc 7B 6
Holly Rd. CO3: S'way 6C 12
Hollytree Ct. CO2: Colc 1J 21
Hollytrees Mus. 4C 42 (4B 14)
Holly Way CO5: Tip 5G 39
      CO7: Elm M 5D 16
Holman Cres. CO3: Colc 7G 13
Holman Rd. CO9: Hals 4B 38
Holmbrook Way CO13: Frin S 5C 28
Holmes Rd. CO9: Hals 5B 38
Holm Oak Cl. CO2: Colc 1C 22
Holmwood Cl. CO16: Clac S 5E 30
Holt Dr. CO2: Colc 5C 22
Holyrood CO12: Har 5E 26
Holy Trinity Church
      Colchester 5B 42
Home Farm La. CO7: A'lgh 1E 8
Homefield Rd. CO2: Colc 3J 21
Homelands Ct. CO14: Walt 3E 28
Homerton Cl. CO15: Clac S 3J 31
Homestead Gdns. CO15: Clac S 5H 31
Honeycroft CO11: Law 4D 10
Honey Pot Hall CO15: Clac S 1K 35
Honeysuckle Way CO4: Colc 3G 15
Honeywood Rd. CO9: Hals 2D 38
Honorius Dr. CO4: Colc 4D 6
Honywood Cl. CO6: M Tey 3C 18
Honywood Rd. CO3: Colc 5K 13
Honywood Way CO13: Kir C 3D 28
Hooper Av. CO2: Colc 3A 22
Hopkins Cl. CO13: Kir C 4D 28
Hopper Wlk. CO4: Colc 5F 15
Hordle Pl. CO12: Har 3J 27
Hordle St. CO12: Har 3J 27
Horkesley Rd. CO4: Boxt 2K 5
Horley Cl. CO16: Clac S 5F 31
Hornbeam Cl. CO2: Colc 2K 21
Hornbeams, The CO12: L Oak 7A 26
Horrocks Cl. CO2: Colc 7C 14
Horse Pond Cl. CO10: Gt Cor 7J 37
Horsey Rd. CO13: Kir S 2A 28
Hospital La. CO3: Colc 5K 13
Hospital Rd. CO3: Colc 5K 13
Howard Av. CO12: Har 5E 26
Howard Rd. CO15: Hol S 7B 32
Howards Cft. CO4: Colc 5K 5
Howard Vyse Ct. CO15: Clac S 6H 31
Howe Chase CO9: Hals 1B 38
Howe Cl. CO4: Colc 4F 15
Hoxter Way CO10: Sud 1E 36
Hoxton Cl. CO16: Clac S 6G 31
Hubbards Chase CO14: Walt 2F 29
Hubert Rd. CO3: Colc 3H 13
Hucklesbury Av. CO15: Hol S 4D 32
Hudson Cl. CO12: Har 6F 27
      CO16: Clac S 6F 31
Hugh Dickson Rd. CO4: Colc 1A 14
Hughes Stanton Way CO11: Law 3D 10
Humber Av. CO15: Jay 6B 34
Humphry Rd. CO2: Colc 3E 36
Hungerdown La. CO7: A'lgh, Law 3G 9
      CO11: Law 3G 9
Hunt Dr. CO16: Clac S 6G 31

Hunter Dr. CO11: Law 4D 10
Hunters Cnr. CO3: Colc 6F 13
Hunters Ridge CO4: Colc 6D 6
Huntingdon Way CO15: Clac S 5H 31
Hunting Ga. CO1: Colc 4E 14
Hunt Way CO13: Kir C 4C 28
Hunwicke Rd. CO4: Colc 4G 15
Hurnard Dr. CO3: Colc 4G 13
Hurrell Down CO4: Colc 6C 6
Hurst Cl. CO7: B'sea 6J 41
HURST GREEN 6J 41
Hussar Cl. CO2: Colc 6A 14
Hutchinson Cl. CO5: Tip 6H 39
Hutley Dr. CO4: Colc 1A 14
Hutleys East Cvn. Pk. CO16: St O 5A 34
Huxtables La. CO3: Ford H 2A 12
Hyacinth Cl. CO16: Clac S 7F 31
Hyams Wlk. CO2: Colc 6B 42 (5B 14)
Hyderabad Cl. CO6: M Tey 6C 14
Hyde Rd. CO10: Sud 4E 36
HYTHE, THE 6E 14
Hythe Cl. CO15: Clac S 4G 35
Hythe Ct. CO7: B'sea 3G 41
Hythe Hill CO1: Colc 5E 14
Hythe Quay CO1: Colc 5E 14
Hythe Station (Rail) 5F 15
Hythe Sta. Rd. CO2: Colc 5F 15

I

Iceni Way CO2: Colc 1H 21
Ilex Cl. CO2: Colc 2K 21
Imogen Cl. CO4: Colc 4H 15
Imperial Ct. CO1: Colc 1A 42 (2A 14)
      CO15: Clac S 3H 35
Imphal Cl. CO2: Colc 3J 21
Ingarfield Rd. CO15: Hol S 5D 32
Ingestre St. CO12: Har 3J 27
Inglenook CO15: Clac S 4K 31
Inglis Rd. CO3: Colc 5K 13
Ingrams Piece CO7: A'lgh 2C 8
Ingram's Well Rd. CO10: Sud 4F 37
Inkerman Row CO10: Sud 3E 36
Inverness Cl. CO1: Colc 3D 42 (3C 14)
Inworth Wlk. CO2: Colc 3C 22
Iona Wlk. CO5: Rhdge 4H 23
Ipswich Rd. CO1: Colc 4D 14
      CO4: Colc 3D 14
      CO7: A'lgh 2G 7
      CO11: Catt 2D 10
      CO15: Hol S 5C 32
Ireton Rd. CO3: Colc 6K 13
Iron Latch La. CO3: Colc 3C 12
Iron Latch Nature Reserve 3C 12
Ironside Wlk. CO11: Law 3E 10
Irvine Rd. CO3: Colc 6J 13
Isbourne Rd. CO4: Colc 4H 15
Island La. CO13: Kir S, Walt 2C 28
Island Rd. CO13: Kir S 1C 28
Ivor Brown Cl. CO4: Colc 6D 6
Ivy Lodge Rd. CO6: Gt Hork 2J 5

J

Jack Andrews Dr. CO4: Colc 5E 6
Jackdaw Dr. CO3: S'way 7B 12
Jack Hatch Way CO7: W'hoe 1J 23
Jackson Ho. CO4: Colc 4D 6
                   (off Honorius Dr.)
      CO15: Clac S 2H 35
Jackson Rd. CO15: Clac S 2H 35
Jackson Wlk. CO2: Colc 7D 14
Jacobs Cl. CO10: Gt Cor 6H 37
Jacqueline Ct. CO3: Colc 4G 13
                  (off Lexden Rd.)
Jade Gdns. CO4: Colc 1B 14
James Carter Rd. CO3: Colc 1E 26
James Cl. CO7: W'hoe 1A 24
James Gore Dr. CO2: Colc 3B 22
James Ho. CO7: B'sea 7G 41
Jameson Pl. CO10: Sud 3E 36
Jameson Rd. CO15: Clac S 1F 35
James Parnell Dr. CO2: Colc 3B 22
James Pl. CO4: Colc 3D 6
James Rd. CO15: Clac S 2F 35
James St. CO1: Colc 7E 42 (5C 14)
      CO7: B'sea 6H 41
Jamestown Cl. CO12: Har 3F 27
James Wicks Cl. CO3: Colc 4A 14
Japonica Cl. CO15: Clac S 7B 32
Jarmin Rd. CO1: Colc 2B 42 (3B 14)
Jasmine Cl. CO4: Colc 3F 15
Jasmine Way CO15: Jay 5D 34

Jays, The CO4: Colc 7D 6
Jays La. CO6: M Tey 3D 18
JAYWICK 4D 34
Jaywick La. CO15: Clac S, Jay 7D 30
      CO16: Clac S 7D 30
Jefferson Cl. CO3: Colc 6E 12
Jeffrey Cl. CO3: Colc 6F 13
Jennings Cl. CO1: Colc 5E 14
Jessica Cl. CO4: Colc 4H 15
Jessop Cl. CO15: Clac S 3K 31
John Ball Wlk. CO1: Colc 4B 42 (4B 14)
John Belcher Wlk. CO4: Colc 5G 15
John Bird Cl. CO1: Colc 1B 42
JOHN DE BOIS HILL 6K 7
John Hammond Cl. CO2: Colc 3B 22
John Harper St. CO1: Colc 2A 42 (3A 14)
John Kavannah Ct. CO1: Colc 6E 42
John Kent Av. CO2: Colc 2H 21
John King Cl. CO7: B'sea 6H 41
John Lawrence Wlk. CO2: Colc 3B 22
                (off William Harris Way)
John Mace Rd. CO2: Colc 3B 22
Johnson's Dr. CO7: Elm M 5E 16
Johnston Cl. CO9: Hals 5C 38
      CO15: Hol S 6D 32
John St. CO7: B'sea 6H 41
Jonagold Dr. CO6: Gt Hork 2H 5
Jonquil Way CO4: Colc 1J 13
Jordan Ct. CO2: Colc 6C 14
Jovian Way CO4: Colc 4D 6
Joyce Brooks Ho. CO3: Colc 5K 13
                     (off Oxford Rd.)
Joy Clucas Ho. CO4: Colc 1J 13
Jubilee Av. CO16: Clac S 4H 31
Jubilee Cl. CO3: S'way 4D 12
      CO12: Har 5D 26
Jubilee Ct. CO1: Colc 1A 42
Jubilee End CO11: Law 2E 10
Jubilee La. CO7: Crock H 7A 8
Jubilee Mdw. CO6: Eig G 3A 12
Jubilee Rd. CO10: Sud 3F 37
Jubilee Way CO13: Frin S 4D 28
Julian Av. CO4: Colc 4D 6
Juniper Cl. CO3: S'way 6C 12
      CO9: Hals 5A 38
Juniper Cl. CO15: Clac S 7J 31
Juniper Rd. CO3: S'way 6C 12
Juniper Way CO4: Colc 3F 15
Juno M. CO2: Colc 3J 21

K

Kale Cft. CO3: S'way 6D 12
Kane M. CO1: Colc 3A 42
Kayla Ct. CO3: Colc 6A 42 (5A 14)
Keable Rd. CO6: M Tey 3C 18
Keating Cl. CO11: Law 3D 10
Keats Rd. CO3: Colc 5F 13
Keble Cl. CO3: Colc 5K 13
Keble Ct. CO5: Tip 5J 39
Keelars La. CO7: W'hoe 3B 24
Keelers Way CO6: Gt Hork 3H 5
Keel Point CO2: Colc 6F 15
Keene Cl. CO5: W Mer 4D 40
Keepers Grn. CO4: Colc 7H 5
Keith Cl. CO15: Clac S 3A 32
Kelso Cl. CO6: Gt Hork 4J 5
Kelvedon Rd. CO5: Inw, Tip 3F 39
      CO5: Mess 1F 39
Kelvin Ct. CO13: Frin S 7D 28
Kempson Dr. CO10: Gt Cor 6H 37
Ken Cooke Ct. CO1: Colc 4B 42 (4B 14)
Kendall Rd. CO1: Colc 7E 42 (5C 14)
Kendall Rd. Folley CO1: Colc 7E 42 (5C 14)
Kendall Ter. CO1: Colc 7D 42 (5C 14)
Kenilworth Rd. CO15: Hol S 5D 32
Kennedy Way CO15: Clac S 6K 31
Kensington Rd. CO2: Colc 6K 13
Kent Cl. CO7: B'sea 5H 41
Kentmere Ct. CO4: Colc 7G 7
Kent's Av. CO15: Hol S 5D 32
Kerridge's Cut CO11: Mist 3J 11
Kerry Ct. CO4: Colc 4E 14
Kersey Av. CO10: Gt Cor 5H 37
Kersey Cl. CO4: Colc 1J 21
Kersey Dr. CO16: Clac S 6E 30
Kestrel Ri. CO9: Hals 4C 38
Kestrel Way CO15: Clac S 5J 31
Keswick Av. CO15: Clac S 5B 32
Keswick Cl. CO13: Kir C 3D 28
Ketley Cl. CO5: Tip 4J 39
Kettle St. CO4: Colc 7B 6
Keymer Way CO3: Colc 7F 13
Keynes Way CO12: Har 4E 26

Key Rd. CO15: Clac S 1H 35
Kilburn Gdns. CO16: Clac S 6G 31
Kildermorie Cl. CO4: Colc 7F 7
Kilmaine Rd. CO12: Har 5E 26
Kiln Barn Av. CO15: Clac S 4J 31
Kiln Dr. CO10: Gt Cor 5H 37
Kiln La. CO11: Mann 3F 11
Kiltie Rd. CO5: Tip 5J 39
Kimberley Rd. CO1: Colc 6D 14
King Charles Rd. CO5: W Mer 5D 40
King Coel Rd. CO3: Colc 4D 12
King Cole Pl. CO4: Colc 2D 14
King Edward Quay CO2: Colc 6F 15
Kingfisher Cl. CO4: Colc 3H 15
Kingfisher Dr. CO12: Har 6D 26
Kingfisher Leisure Cen.
     Sudbury 5F 37
Kingfisher Mdws. CO9: Hals 4C 38
Kingfishers CO10: Sud 5D 36
    CO15: Clac S 5J 31
King George Rd. CO2: Colc 7B 14
King George's Av. CO12: Har 3G 27
King Harold Rd. CO3: Colc 7G 13
Kings Av. CO15: Hol S 6B 32
Kingsbury CO6: M Tey 3D 18
Kingsbury Wlk. CO10: Gt Cor 6J 37
                    (off Kempson Dr.)
Kings Ol. CO11: Law 3E 10
Kings Ct. CO4: Colc 4D 6
    CO5: Tip 3G 39
    CO12: Har 4G 27
    CO15: Hol S 6C 32
Kings Ford Ct. CO2: Colc 1H 21
Kings Head Ct. CO1: Colc ...1A 42 (4B 14)
King's Head St. CO12: Har 1J 27
Kings Hill CO10: Gt Cor 5G 37
Kingsland Beach CO5: W Mer 6C 40
Kingsland Cl. CO5: W Mer 6C 40
Kingsland Hgts. CO5: W Mer 5C 40
Kingsland Rd. CO5: W Mer 6C 40
Kingsman Dr. CO16: Clac S 6F 31
Kings Mdw. CO10: Gt Cor 5G 37
Kings Mdw. Rd. CO1: Colc ...2B 42 (3B 14)
Kingsmere Cl. CO5: W Mer 5D 40
Kings M. CO7: W'hoe 7A 16
Kings Pde. CO15: Clac S 3H 35
    CO15: Hol S 7B 32
Kings Quay St. CO12: Har 1K 27
                    (not continuous)
King's Rd. CO12: Har 4G 27
    CO15: Clac S 3G 35
Kings Rd. CO9: Hals 4B 38
King Stephen Rd. CO1: Colc 5D 14
Kingston M. CO15: Clac S 1F 35
King St. CO10: Sud 4E 36
Kingsway CO5: Tip 4G 39
    CO12: Har 3J 27
Kingswood Rd. CO4: Colc 6B 6
Kingwell Av. CO15: Clac S 6H 31
Kinlett Cl. CO4: Colc 6D 6
Kino Rd. CO14: Walt 2H 29
KIRBY CROSS 4A 28
KIRBY-LE-SOKEN 2B 28
Kirby Rd. CO14: Walt 2D 28
Kirkbaye CO13: Kir C 4C 28
Kirkhurst Cl. CO7: B'sea 6J 41
Kirk Way CO4: Colc 4C 6
Kitchen Hill CO10: Bulm, Sud 4A 36
Knevett Cl. CO4: Colc 7A 6
Knightsbridge Cl. CO2: Colc 1J 21
Knightsbridge Ct. CO15: Clac S 7A 32
                (off Connaught Gdns. E.)
Knights Cl. CO5: Tip 7K 39
    CO11: Law 3E 10
Knights Fld. CO2: Colc 6C 14
Knowles Cl. CO9: Hals 4B 38
Knox Gdns. CO15: Clac S 6H 31
Knox Ct. CO15: Clac S 6H 31
Knox Rd. CO15: Clac S 6H 31
Kohima Rd. CO2: Colc 3H 21
Kreswell Gro. CO12: Har 5G 27

L

Laburnum Cl. CO15: Clac S 1F 35
Laburnum Cres. CO13: Kir C 4B 28
Laburnum Gro. CO4: Colc 3G 15
Ladbrook Dr. CO2: Colc 1C 22
Ladbrooke Rd. CO16: Clac S 5G 31
Ladell Cl. CO3: Colc 1E 20
Ladysmith Av. CO7: B'sea 5G 41
Laing Rd. CO4: Colc 5G 15
Lake Av. CO15: Clac S 1F 35
Lakeside Cvn. Pk. CO7: B'sea 6G 41

Lakeside Wlk. CO3: S'way 7C 12
Lake Wlk. CO15: Clac S 1F 35
Lake Way CO15: Jay 6C 34
Lambeth Rd. CO2: Colc 7K 13
Lambeth Wlk. CO15: Clac S 6H 31
Lambourne Cl. CO3: S'way 7D 12
    CO15: Clac S 3J 31
Lammas Way CO7: W'hoe 2A 24
Lampon Cl. CO6: W Ber 6E 4
Lancaster App. CO7: Colc 5F 7
Lancaster Ct. CO13: Frin S 5E 28
Lancaster Gdns. E. CO15: Clac S 7K 31
Lancaster Gdns. W.
Lancaster Rd. CO10: Sud 1D 36
Lancer St. CO2: Colc 7K 13
Lanchester Av. CO15: Jay 6A 34
Lancia Av. CO15: Jay 6B 34
Land Cl. CO16: Clac S 6F 31
Land La. CO1: Colc 4D 42 (4C 14)
Landsdown Rd. CO10: Sud 2G 37
Landseer Ct. CO15: Clac S 2J 35
Landseer Rd. CO3: Colc 6H 13
    CO15: Clac S 3J 31
Lane, The CO5: W Mer 4A 40
    CO11: Mist 3H 11
    CO15: Clac S 1F 35
Langdale Dr. CO4: Colc 6D 6
Langham Dr. CO16: Clac S 7E 30
Langham La. CO4: Boxt, L'ham 2C 6
Langham Lodge La.
    CO4: L'ham 2G 7
Langham Pl. CO4: Colc 7D 6
Langham Rd. CO4: Boxt 1B 6
Langley Cl. CO4: Colc 4H 27
Langtry Ct. CO15: Clac S 2K 35
                (off Thoroughfare Rd.)
Languidic Cl. CO10: Gt Cor 5J 37
Langwood CO5: W Mer 4C 40
Lansdowne Cl. CO5: Tip 4G 39
Lanswood Pk. CO7: Elm M 7G 17
Lanvalley Rd. CO3: Colc 5E 12
Larch Cl. CO4: Colc 3F 15
Lark Ri. CO10: Ball 6D 36
Larksfield Cres.
    CO13: Kir C 4C 28
Lark Way CO13: Kir C 3C 28
Larneys, The CO13: Kir C 3C 28
Lathe Ct. CO4: Colc 5F 15
Launceston Cl. CO2: Colc 3D 22
Laurel Av. CO12: Har 5E 26
Laurel Cl. CO15: Clac S 4A 32
Laurel Ct. CO4: Colc 3G 15
                    (off Magnolia Dr.)
Laurels, The CO13: Gt Hol 4A 28
Laurence Cl. CO7: Elm M 5D 16
Lavender Cl. CO5: Tip 6G 39
Lavender Wlk. CO15: Jay 5D 34
Lavender Way CO4: Colc 1J 13
Lavenham Cl. CO16: Clac S 7E 30
Lovenham Cl. CO2: Colc 2J 21
                    (off Layer Rd.)
LAWFORD 4D 10
Lawford Pl. CO11: Law 4C 10
Lawns Cl. CO5: W Mer 4C 40
Laxton Cl. CO15: Clac S 7G 13
Laxton Rd. CO7: Alr 4F 25
Layer Ct. CO2: Colc 7K 13
Layer Cross CO2: Lay H 7F 21
LAYER-DE-LA-HAYE 7F 21
Layer Rd. CO2: Colc 6H 21
    CO5: Abb 7A 22
Layzell Cft. CO10: Gt Cor 6J 37
Leam Cl. CO4: Colc 4H 15
Leas, The CO13: Frin S 4F 29
Lea Side CO5: W Mer 5D 40
Leas La. CO2: B'ch 6D 20
Leas Rd. CO2: Colc 3J 21
    CO15: Clac S 5C 6
Le Cateau Rd. CO2: Colc 7A 42 (5A 14)
                    (not continuous)
Leech's La. CO4: Colc 6K 5
Lee Rd. CO12: Har 4H 27
Legerton Dr. CO16: Clac S 6D 30
Leicester Cl. CO1: Colc 3D 42 (3C 14)
    CO15: Jay 3C 34
Leisure World
    Colchester 1D 42 (2C 14)
    Highwoods 5D 6
    Tiptree 3H 39
Leisure World Tennis Cen. 7J 13
Lenz Cl. CO1: Colc 5E 14
Leonard Pl. CO1: Colc 1A 42
Les Bois CO2: Lay H 7G 21
Letches La. CO9: Hals 7A 38

Lethe Gro. CO2: Colc 4B 22
Lewis Gdns. CO1: Colc 5D 42 (4C 14)
Lewis Rd. CO16: Clac S 5D 30
LEXDEN 5F 13
Lexden Ct. CO3: Colc 4J 13
Lexden Earthworks 5E 12
Lexden Gathering Grounds Nature Reserve
    ....4F 13
Lexden Gro. CO3: Colc 4F 13
Lexden M. CO3: Colc 4F 13
Lexden Pk. CO3: Colc 5G 13
Lexden Rd. CO3: Colc 4E 12
Lexden Raquets & Fitness Club 4D 12
Lexden Springs Local Nature Reserve
    ....4G 13
Lexden Wood Golf Course 2G 13
Ley Fld. CO6: M Tey 3C 18
Leys Dr. CO16: L Cla 2F 31
Leys Rd. CO7: W'hoe 1A 24
Leyton Ct. CO15: Clac S 3J 31
Libius Dr. CO4: Colc 5C 6
Lichfield Cl. CO1: Colc 3E 42 (3C 14)
Lifeboat Station
    Harwich 1K 27
Lightship Way CO2: Colc 6F 15
Lilac Ct. CO7: W'hoe 2J 23
Lilac Tree Ct. CO4: Colc 3G 15
Lilian Impey Dr. CO4: Colc 5D 6
Lilley's La. CO7: Gt Bro 6G 9
Lime Av. CO4: Colc 3F 15
    CO12: Har 4G 27
Lime Cl. CO15: Clac S 1F 35
Lime Ct. CO12: Har 4G 27
Lime Gro. CO10: Ball 6C 36
Limes, The CO7: A'lgh 3D 8
Lime St. CO7: B'sea 7H 41
Lincoln Av. CO15: Jay 6A 34
Lincoln La. CO6: Gt Hork 1J 5
Lincoln Way
    CO1: Colc 4E 42 (4C 14)
    CO4: Colc 2G 15
    CO11: Law 4D 10
Linden Dr. CO15: Clac S 4H 31
Lindens, The CO9: Hals 5C 38
Lindsey Av. CO10: Gt Cor 5H 37
Lindsey Ct. CO10: Gt Cor 5H 37
Link Cl. CO4: Colc 6A 6
Link Rd. CO7: B'sea 6J 41
    CO9: Hals 5A 38
    CO15: Clac S 2G 35
Linkside CO13: Frin S 7C 28
Linley Gdns. CO15: Clac S 2G 35
Linnet M. CO4: Colc 7B 6
Linnets CO15: Clac S 5J 31
Linstead Cl. CO16: Clac S 7D 30
Lionel Hurst Cl. CO10: Gt Cor 6J 37
Lion Wlk. CO1: Colc 5B 42 (4B 14)
Lion Wlk. Shop. Con. CO1: Colc .5B 42 (4B 14)
Lisle Rd. CO2: Colc 6C 14
Litchfield CO12: Har 5D 26
Litchfield Cl. CO15: Clac S 6H 31
Little Acorns CO4: Colc 6F 7
Little Bakers CO14: Walt 3E 28
Lit. Bromley Rd. CO7: A'lgh 3D 8
    CO7: Gt Bro 7J 9
Littlebury Gdns. CO2: Colc 7E 14
Lit. Church St. CO12: Har 1J 27
                    (off Church St.)
LITTLE CLACTON 1G 31
Lit. Clacton By-Pass CO15: Clac S ..3F 31
    CO16: Clac S, L Cla, Wee H ...1E 30
Lit. Clacton Rd. CO13: Clac S, Gt Hol .1C 32
    CO16: Clac S, L Cla 4E 30
Littlecotes CO4: Colc 6K 5
Littlefield CO7: W'hoe 3A 24
Lit. Wood M. CO4: Colc 1K 13
Littlefield Cl. CO2: Colc 2J 21
Littlefield Rd. CO2: Colc 2J 21
Little Foxburrows CO2: Colc 7A 14
Little Harrods CO14: Walt 3E 28
LITTLE OAKLEY 7B 26
Lit. Stone Ct. CO15: Clac S 4F 35
LITTLE TEY 2A 18
Little Wood CO13: Kir C 4C 28
Lit. Wood M. CO4: Colc 1K 13
Lockhart Av. CO3: Colc 4J 13
Lock Rd. CO9: Hals 5B 38
Lodders Wlk. CO2: Colc 7A 14
Lodge, The CO15: Hol S 5E 32
Lodge Cl. CO12: L Oak 7A 26
    CO15: Clac S 7H 31
Lodge Ct. CO6: W Ber 6F 5
Lodge Farm La. CO16: St O 7A 30

Lodge La. CO4: L'ham 2E 6
    CO7: A'lgh 4A 8
                        (Colchester Rd.)
    CO7: A'lgh 4J 7
                        (Crown La. Nth.)
    CO7: B'sea 5F 41
Lodge Rd. CO7: B'sea 4G 41
    CO12: L Oak 7B 26
    CO16: L Cla 1A 32
Lombardy Rd. CO10: Sud 1D 36
London Rd. CO3: Colc, S'way 2G 19
    CO5: Fee 7A 18
    CO6: Cop, M Tey 7A 18
    CO6: Gt Hork 2E 4
    CO15: Clac S 5H 31
    CO16: Clac S, L Cla 1G 31
Longacre CO4: Colc 1A 14
Longcroft Rd. CO4: Colc 3E 14
Longdryve CO2: Colc 7J 13
                        (not continuous)
Long Grn. CO6: M Tey 3C 18
Long La. CO13: Gt Hol 7A 28
Long Meadows CO12: Har 5D 26
Longridge CO4: Colc 3H 15
Long Rd. CO11: Law, Mist 5D 10
Longstraw Cl. CO3: S'way 5D 12
Long Wyre St. CO1: Colc 5C 42 (4B 14)
Lord Holland Rd. CO2: Colc 1B 22
Lord Nelson Ct. CO7: W'hoe 5A 24
                    (off Walter Radcliffe Rd.)
Lordswood Rd. CO2: Colc 2J 21
Lorkin Way CO6: W Ber 6F 5
Lotts Yd. CO1: Colc 5D 14
Lotus Way CO15: Jay 5B 34
Louise Cl. CO14: Walt 6J 29
Louvain Rd. CO12: Har 6F 27
Love La. CO7: B'sea 4G 41
Love Way CO16: Clac S 5F 31
Lowe Chase CO14: Walt 2F 29
LOWER END 7J 21
Lwr. Farm La. CO7: B'sea 5K 41
Lower Grn. Gdns. CO7: B'sea 6H 41
Lwr. Marine Pde. CO12: Har 5G 27
Lwr. Park Rd. CO7: B'sea 6G 41
Lower Reeve CO10: Gt Cor 7H 37
Lower Rd. CO2: B'ch 7A 20
    CO10: Borl 1B 36
Low Lighthouse (Maritime, National Vintage
    Wireless & Television Mus.) 2K 27
Low Rd. CO12: Har 6D 26
Lucas Ho. CO3: Colc 4G 13
Lucas Rd. CO2: Colc 7D 42 (5B 14)
    CO10: Sud 4F 37
Lucerne Rd. CO7: Elm M 5E 16
Lucius Cres. CO4: Colc 4D 6
Lucy Cl. CO3: S'way 5C 12
Lucy La. Nth. CO3: S'way 4B 12
Lucy La. Sth. CO3: S'way 4C 12
Luff Way CO14: Walt 3D 28
Lufkin Rd. CO4: Colc 7B 6
Lugar Cl. CO4: Colc 5G 15
Lulworth Cl. CO15: Clac S 4F 35
Lumber Leys CO14: Walt 3E 28
Lungley Ri. CO2: Colc 4B 22
Lupin Way CO16: Clac S 7F 31
Lushington Av. CO13: Kir C 4B 28
Lushington Rd. CO11: Law 3E 10
Luther Dr. CO5: Tip 5J 39
Lydgate Cl. CO11: Law 3D 10
Lymington Av. CO15: Clac S 3J 31
Lyndhurst Rd. CO15: Hol S 7B 32
Lynne Cl. CO13: Kir C 4C 28
Lynton Cl. CO12: Har 3G 27
Lyon Cl. CO15: Clac S 7K 31

M

Mabbitt Way CO4: Colc 5D 6
Macbeth Cl. CO4: Colc 4H 15
McCluskeys St. CO4: Colc 7B 6
Mackay Cl. CO2: Colc 3D 22
Madeira Rd. CO15: Hol S 7B 32
Madeley Cl. CO4: Colc 4B 22
Magazine Farm Way CO3: Colc 5G 13
Magdalen Cl. CO15: Clac S 7H 31
Magdalen Grn. CO1: Colc 5D 14
Magdalen Rd. CO15: Clac S 7H 31
Magdalen St. CO1: Colc 6D 42 (5C 14)
Magistrates' Court
    Colchester 6D 42 (5C 14)
Magnolia Dr. CO4: Colc 3G 15
Magnus Dr. CO4: Colc 4D 6
Magpie Chase CO3: S'way 7B 12
Magpie Cl. CO12: Har 6D 26

Maidenburgh St. CO1: Colc 4C 42 (4B 14)
Main Rd. CO6: Wmgfd 1A 4
    CO7: Frat 1K 25
    CO12: Har 3J 27
                            (High St.)
    CO12: Har 5D 26
                            (Oakley Rd.)
    CO12: R'sy 6A 26
    CO13: Gt Hol 1F 33
Makins Rd. CO12: Har 2E 26
Maldon Ct. CO3: Colc 7A 42 (5A 14)
    CO10: Gt Cor 4H 37
                        (not continuous)
Maldon Rd. CO2: B'ch, Heck 7A 20
    CO3: Colc 6J 13
    CO3: Heck, S'way 6A 42 (3B 20)
    CO5: Tip 7F 39
Maldon Way CO16: Clac S 7E 30
Mallard Cl. CO2: Lay H 7G 21
Mallard Way CO10: Gt Cor 6J 37
Mallows Fld. CO9: Hals 3C 38
Malthouse Rd. CO11: Mann 3F 11
Malting Farm La. CO7: A'lgh 1A 8
MALTING GREEN 7H 21
Malting Grn. Rd. CO2: Lay H 7H 21
Malting La. CO13: Kir S 1A 28
Malting Rd. CO2: Colc 3J 21
Maltings Pk. Rd. CO6: W Ber 6F 5
Maltings Rd. CO7: B'sea 4G 41
Maltings Wharf CO11: Mann 3F 11
Malting Yd. CO7: W'hoe 4K 23
Malvern Way CO6: Gt Hork 3H 5
Manchester Rd. CO15: Hol S 5D 32
Mandeville Rd. CO6: M Tey 3C 18
Mandeville Way CO13: Kir C 3D 28
Manfield CO9: Hals 3C 38
MANNINGTREE 3F 11
Manningtree Mus. 3F 11
Manningtree Sports Cen. 3E 10
Manningtree Station (Rail) 2C 10
Manor Cl. CO6: Gt Hork 3J 5
Manor Gdns. CO2: Colc 4K 13
Manor Ho. Way CO7: B'sea 4G 41
Manor La. CO12: Har 5F 27
Manor Pde. CO7: B'sea 5G 41
Manor Rd. CO3: Colc 5A 42 (4K 13)
    CO6: W Ber 5E 4
    CO7: W'hoe 3A 24
    CO10: Sud 2E 36
    CO12: Har 4F 27
Manors Grn. CO9: Hals 5A 38
Manor Way CO15: Hol S 5F 33
Mansion Ho. CO2: Colc 2J 21
Maple Cl. CO9: Hals 3D 38
    CO12: Har 4H 27
    CO15: Clac S 1E 34
Maple Dr. CO13: Kir C 4B 28
Maple Leaf CO5: Tip 3G 39
Maple Rd. CO10: Gt Cor 6H 37
Maple Way CO2: Colc 7C 14
Maplin Ct. CO15: Hol S 7C 32
Marasca End CO2: Colc 5C 22
Maraschino Cres. CO2: Colc 5C 22
Marcus Cl. CO4: Colc 4D 6
Marennes Cres. CO7: B'sea 5G 41
Mareth Rd. CO2: Colc 6J 41
Margaret Cl. CO7: B'sea 5G 41
Margaret Rd. CO1: Colc 2A 42 (3A 14)
Maria Ct. CO2: Colc 6E 14
                            (off Hesper Rd.)
Maria St. CO12: Har 2J 27
Marigold Av. CO16: Clac S 6F 31
Marigold Cl. CO4: Colc 3G 15
Marina Gdns. CO15: Clac S 6B 32
Marina M. CO14: Walt 2G 29
Marina Point CO15: Clac S 3G 35
Marine Cl. CO13: Frin S 6D 28
Marine Ho. CO2: Colc 6F 15
Marine Pde. CO2: Colc 6F 15
Marine Pde. E. CO15: Clac S ...7A 32, 2J 35
Marine Pde. W. CO15: Clac S 3G 35
Marion Av. CO15: Hol S 5H 31
Mario Way CO2: Colc 1B 22
Market Cl. CO1: Colc 3A 42 (3A 14)
Market Hill CO9: Hals 3B 38
    CO10: Sud 4E 36
Market St. CO12: Har 1K 27
MARKS TEY 3C 18
MARKS TEY INTERCHANGE 2F 19
MARKS TEY RDBT. 2E 18
Marks Tey Station (Rail) 2F 19
Marlborough Cl. CO15: Clac S 1F 35
Marlborough Dr. CO10: Sud 3F 37
Marlowe Rd. CO15: Jay 3D 34
Marlowe Way CO3: Colc 5F 13

Marney Way CO13: Frin S 4F 29
Marram Cl. CO3: S'way 5B 12
Marriages Yd. CO1: Colc 4D 14
                            (off East St.)
Marsden Ct. CO3: Colc 7E 12
Marsh Cres. CO5: Rhdge 4J 23
Marsh Farm La. CO7: Alr 5C 24
Marsh La. CO12: Har 7E 26
Marsh Way CO7: B'sea 6G 41
Martello Cvn. Pk. CO14: Walt 1G 29
Martello Holiday Pk. CO14: Walt ...2G 29
Martello Rd. CO14: Walt 2G 29
Martello Tower
    Jaywick 6A 34
    No. 2 ....4G 35
    No. 3 ....5F 35
    Walton-on-the-Naze 1G 29
Martello Twr. Est. CO16: P'nt C 7G 41
Martin End CO2: Lay H 7G 21
Martinsdale CO15: Clac S 5J 31
Martin's Rd. CO9: Hals 4B 38
Martins Rd. CO10: Sud 2H 37
Maryborough Gro. CO2: Colc 2D 22
Maryland Ct. CO2: Colc 3C 22
Mary La. Nth. CO7: Gt Bro 3K 17
Mary Warner Rd. CO7: A'lgh 3C 8
Mascot Ct. CO15: Clac S 6J 31
Mascot Sq. CO4: Colc 6F 15
Masefield Dr. CO3: Colc 5F 13
Mason Cl. CO2: Colc 1H 21
Mason Rd. CO1: Colc 1B 42 (2B 14)
    CO16: Clac S 1E 34
Matchett Dr. CO4: Colc 4D 6
Mathews Cl. CO9: Hals 2D 38
Maudlyn Rd. CO1: Colc 5E 14
Maximus Dr. CO4: Colc 4D 6
Mayberry Wlk. CO2: Colc 1C 22
Maybury Cl. CO6: M Tey 3D 18
Mayda Cl. CO9: Hals 4A 38
Mayes La. CO12: R'sy 6A 26
Mayfair Ct. CO2: Colc 7E 14
Mayfield Cl. CO2: Colc 2E 14
Mayflower Av. CO12: Har 2K 27
Mayflower Cl. CO3: S'way 5D 12
Mayflower Ho. CO12: Har 3F 27
                        (off Williamsburg Av.)
Mayflower Way CO10: Sud 1F 37
Mayford Way CO16: Clac S 5E 30
Mayor's Wlk. CO1: Colc 4C 42 (4B 14)
MAYPOLE GREEN 3J 21
Maypole Grn. Rd. CO2: Colc 3J 21
Maypole Rd. CO5: Tip 4G 39
Meachen Rd. CO2: Colc 6E 14
Mead, The CO7: B'sea 4H 41
    CO10: Gt Cor 7H 37
Meadowbrook Ct. CO1: Colc 4D 14
Meadow Cl. CO7: Elm M 5D 16
    CO7: Gt Bro 5K 17
    CO9: Hals 5C 38
    CO15: Clac S 4A 32
Meadowcroft Way CO13: Kir C 3D 28
Meadow Grass Cl. CO3: S'way 5B 12
Meadow Grn. CO5: W Mer 6C 40
    CO10: Sud 5E 36
Meadow Pl. CO10: Sud 5E 36
Meadow Rd. CO2: Colc 3K 21
    CO10: Sud 4E 36
Meadowview CO5: Tip 5F 39
Meadowview Holiday Pk. CO16: L Cla ..2E 30
Meadow Vw. Cl. CO3: S'way 6E 12
Meadow Vw. Rd. CO10: Ball 5D 36
Meadow Way CO15: Jay 4D 34
Meadway CO11: Law 4C 10
Meander M. CO1: Colc 1E 42 (2C 14)
Mede Way CO7: W'hoe 1A 24
Medusa Ct. CO12: Har 5G 27
Meekings Rd. CO10: Sud 3H 37
Meers, The CO13: Kir C 5D 28
Melbourne Chase CO2: Colc 3D 22
Melbourne Rd. CO15: Clac S 7G 31
Melford Rd. CO10: Sud 1C 36
Mellor Chase CO3: Colc 4E 12
Melrose Gdns. CO15: Clac S 6B 32
Melrose Rd. CO5: W Mer 5C 40
Melso Cl. CO10: Gt Cor 6G 37
Melton Cl. CO16: Clac S 7D 30
Memnon Ct. CO2: Colc 1B 22
Mendlesham Cl. CO16: Clac S 7E 30
Menin Rd. CO2: Colc 7K 13
Meopham Ct. CO2: Colc 7D 14
                            (off Stalin Rd.)
Mercers Way CO1: Colc 2A 42 (3A 14)
Mercury Cl. CO2: Colc 1G 21
Mercury Theatre
    Colchester 5A 42 (4A 14)

Meredith Rd. CO15: Clac S 1H 35
Merediths Cl. CO7: W'hoe 4J 23
Meriden Ct. CO15: Clac S 5K 31
Merivale Cl. CO11: Law 4E 10
Merivale Rd. CO11: Law 4D 10
Merlin End CO4: Colc 2H 15
Merrilees Cres. CO15: Hol S 5C 32
Merrymount Gdns. CO15: Clac S 6A 32
Mersea Av. CO5: W Mer 5B 40
Mersea Ct. CO5: W Mer 4B 40
Mersea Island Mus. 5B 40
Mersea Rd. CO2: Colc 4D 22
  (Cabbage Hall La.)
CO2: Colc 7C 42 (5B 14)
  (Cromwell Rd.)
Merstham Dr. CO16: Clac S 5F 31
Merton Ct. CO2: Colc 5C 22
Messines Rd. CO2: Colc 7K 13
MESSING 1G 39
Messing Rd. CO5: Tip 3G 39
Mews, The CO5: W Mer 4D 40
CO12: Har 4H 27
CO13: Frin S 6D 28
  (Old Rd.)
CO13: Frin S 5F 28
  (Peacehaven)
Mews Ct. CO11: Mist 3J 11
Meyrick Cres. CO2: Colc 6B 14
Michaelstowe Cl. CO12: Har 5B 26
Michaelstowe Dr. CO12: Har 5B 26
Middleborough CO1: Colc 3A 42 (3A 14)
  (not continuous)
Middlefield CO9: Hals 4C 38
Middlefield Rd. CO11: Mist 4D 10
Middle Mill Rd. CO1: Colc 3B 42 (3B 14)
MIDDLETON 7E 36
Middleton Cl. CO16: Clac S 5G 31
Middleton Hall Cotts. CO10: Midd 6E 36
Middleton Rd. CO10: Ball, Midd 5C 36
Middlewick Cl. CO2: Colc 3C 22
Midland Cl. CO2: Colc 7B 14
Midway CO15: Jay 6A 34
Midway Rd. CO2: Colc 2J 21
MILE END 6A 6
Mile End Rd. CO4: Colc 7K 5
Miles Cl. CO3: S'way 5C 12
Milford Cl. CO7: W'hoe 3A 24
Military Ct. CO1: Colc 7E 42 (5C 14)
Military Rd. CO1: Colc 6D 42 (5C 14)
Military Way CO12: Har 5B 26
Mill Apartments, The CO1: Colc 4D 14
Mill Bri. CO9: Hals 4B 38
Mill Chase CO9: Hals 3B 38
Mill Cl. CO5: Tip 4G 39
CO12: Har 3H 27
Millcroft M. CO5: W Mer 4C 40
Millers Barn Golf Course 3D 34
Miller's Barn Rd. CO15: Jay 3D 34
Millers Cl. CO3: S'way 5C 12
CO6: Gt Hork 3H 5
Millers La. CO3: S'way 5D 12
Millers Reach CO11: Mist 3H 11
Millfields CO2: Lay H 7J 21
CO5: Tip 4G 39
Mill Grn. CO9: Hals 3B 38
Mill Hill CO10: Sud 4D 36
CO11: Law 3A 10
CO11: Law, Mist 3E 10
Mill La. CO2: Lay H 7H 21
CO7: A'lgh, Gt Bro 6F 9
CO10: Sud 4D 36
CO11: Law, Mist 3F 11
CO12: Har 3J 27
CO13: Gt Hol 1D 32
CO14: Walt 1G 29
Mill Rd. CO4: Colc 6A 6
CO5: W Mer 4C 40
CO6: M Tey 2G 19
Mills Rd. CO10: Sud 3G 37
Millstone Grn. CO6: Cop 2H 19
Mill St. CO1: Colc 7D 42 (6B 14)
CO7: B'sea 6J 41
Mill Tye CO10: Gt Cor 7G 37
Mill Wlk. CO5: Tip 4G 39
Millwrights CO5: Tip 4G 39
Milner Rd. CO10: Sud 3H 37
Milton Cl. CO3: Colc 5F 13
Milton Rd. CO11: Law 5D 10
CO12: Har 3J 27
Mimosa Ct. CO4: Colc 3G 15
Minden Rd. CO10: Sud 4F 37
Minerva Cl. CO12: Har 6E 26
Minerva End CO2: Colc 3J 21
Minories Art Gallery 5C 42 (4C 14)
Minsmere Dr. CO16: Clac S 5F 31

Minsmere Way CO10: Gt Cor 5J 37
Miranda Wlk. CO4: Colc 4G 15
MISTLEY 3H 11
MISTLEY HEATH 5K 11
Mistley Place Pk. 3G 11
Mistley Station (Rail) 3H 11
Mistley Towers 2H 11
Mitchell Av. CO9: Hals 5B 38
Modlen Rd. CO14: Walt 3E 28
Monarch La. CO6: Gt Hork 3H 5
Monklands Ct. CO9: Hals 4A 38
Monkwick Av. CO2: Colc 2B 22
Monkwick Ct. CO9: Hals 4A 38
Monkwick Sports Cen. 2B 22
Mons Rd. CO2: Colc 7K 13
Montbretia Cl. CO3: S'way 5D 12
Montbretia Ct. CO16: Clac S 7F 31
Montgomery Cl. CO2: Colc 7D 14
Moorhouse Grn. CO7: A'lgh 2C 8
Moorsfield CO10: Gt Cor 7H 37
Moorside CO1: Colc 4D 14
Moorside Bus. Pk. CO1: Colc 4D 14
Morant Rd. CO1: Colc 6D 14
Morebarn Rd. CO7: Gt Bro 1J 17
Morello Ct. CO2: Colc 5C 22
Morland Ct. CO6: Gt Hork 1H 5
Morley Rd. CO5: Tip 6H 39
  (Halo)
CO9: Halo 3C 38
Morris Av. CO15: Jay 6B 34
Morrow La. CO7: A'lgh 4E 8
Morses La. CO7: B'sea 4H 41
Morten Rd. CO1: Colc 2A 42 (3A 14)
Mortimer Ct. CO1: Colc 5B 42
Mortimer Gdns. CO4: Colc 4D 6
Morton Way CO9: Hals 2D 38
Mossfield Cl. CO3: Colc 5J 13
Moss Rd. CO3: S'way 7E 12
Moss Way CO6: W Ber 7E 4
Motor Wlk. CO4: Colc 1J 13
Mott's La. CO6: M Tey 2B 18
Moulton Cl. CO10: Sud 3F 37
Mount, The CO3: Colc 5F 13
Mountain Ash Cl. CO4: Colc 1E 14
Mountbatten Cl. CO10: Sud 1F 37
Mountbatten Dr. CO2: Colc 1D 22
Mountbatten Rd. CO10: Sud 1F 37
Mount Hill CO9: Hals 5A 38
Mt. Pleasant CO9: Hals 4B 38
Mount Ri. CO9: Hals 4A 38
Mountview Rd. CO15: Clac S 6K 31
Moverons La. CO7: B'sea 3F 41
Moy Rd. CO2: Colc 3C 22
Mulberry Av. CO2: Colc 7C 14
Mulberry Bus. Cen. CO2: Colc 7F 15
Mulberry Harbour Way CO7: W'hoe 4K 23
Mulberry Wlk. CO5: Tip 7H 39
Mumford Cl. CO6: W Ber 6E 4
Mumford Rd. CO6: W Ber 7D 4
Mumfords La. CO13: Kir C, Kir S 1A 28
Munnings Dr. CO16: Clac S 5G 31
Munnings Rd. CO3: Colc 6G 13
Munnings Way CO11: Law 2D 10
Muscade Cl. CO5: Tip 4H 39
Museum St. CO1: Colc 5C 42 (4B 14)
Musgrave Cl. CO12: Har 6E 26
Musk Cl. CO3: S'way 4D 12
Muswell Wlk. CO16: Clac S 6G 31
Myland Hall Chase CO4: Colc 7E 6
Mynott Ct. CO5: Tip 6H 39
Myrtle Gro. CO2: Colc 6D 14
Mytchett Cl. CO16: Clac S 5E 30

N

Nancy Smith Cl. CO2: Colc 6B 14
Nansen Rd. CO15: Hol S 5C 32
Napier Av. CO15: Jay 6A 34
Napier Rd. CO2: Colc 7B 42 (5B 14)
Nash Cl. CO3: Colc 6H 13
CO11: Law 2D 10
Nathan Ct. CO2: Colc 4D 22
Nayland Dr. CO16: Clac S 7E 30
Nayland Rd. CO4: Colc 5K 5
CO6: Gt Hork 3J 5
CO6: W Ber 4D 4
NAZE, THE 7H 29
Nazecliff Gdns. CO14: Walt 6J 29
Naze Ct. CO14: Walt 6J 29
Naze Marine Holiday Pk. ....
CO14: Walt 7H 29
Naze Pk. Rd. CO14: Walt 7H 29
Naze Twr., The 6J 29
Neale Rd. CO9: Hals 4B 38
Neasden Av. CO16: Clac S 6G 31
Nelson Cl. CO7: W'hoe 2A 24

Nelson Rd. CO3: Colc 4E 12
CO10: Sud 2G 37
CO12: Har 3H 27
CO15: Clac S 3H 35
Nelson St. CO7: B'sea 7G 41
Neptune Ct. CO1: Colc 5E 14
  (off Hythe Hill)
Nesfield Rd. CO4: Colc 6H 15
Nether Ct. CO9: Hals 4D 38
New Barley Store, The ....
CO11: Mist 3H 11
Newbridge Hill CO3: Colc 1D 12
CO6: W Ber 1D 12
Newbridge Rd. CO5: Tip, Lay M 5J 39
New Captains Rd. CO5: W Mer 5B 40
Newcastle Av. CO3: Colc 7E 12
New Church Rd. CO6: W Ber 6D 4
Newcomen Way CO4: Colc 4D 6
New Cut CO2: Lay H 7F 21
New Farm Rd. CO3: S'way 5D 12
Newgate St. CO1: Walt 2G 29
New Hall Lodge Pk. CO12: Har 6F 27
Newhaven La. CO12: Har 1J 27
  (off George St.)
Newhythe CO3: Colc 4F 12
New Kiln Rd. CO3: Colc 4J 13
Newington Gdns. CO15: Clac S 3J 31
Newman Rd. CO2: Colc 7K 13
Newman's Rd. CO10: Sud 3E 36
NEW MISTLEY 3K 11
New Orleans Flats CO5: W Mer 6B 40
New Pk. Gdns. CO7: B'sea 5H 41
New Pk. St. CO1: Colc 5D 14
New Pier St. CO14: Walt 2G 29
Newport Cl. CO12: Har 6F 27
Newport Dr. CO15: Clac S 4K 31
Newport Way CO13: Frin S 4E 28
New Queens Rd. CO10: Sud 2E 36
New Rd. CO3: S'way 5D 12
CO5: Mess 1G 39
CO5: Tip 5H 39
CO11: Mann, Mist 4F 11
New St. CO7: B'sea 7H 41
CO9: Hals 4A 38
CO10: Sud 3E 36
Newton Cft. CO10: Sud 4G 37
Newton Ho. CO2: Colc 6A 14
Newton Rd. CO10: Gt Cor, Sud 4F 37
CO12: Har 4F 27
New Town Rd. CO1: Colc 7E 42 (5C 14)
Nexus, The CO1: Colc 3A 42
NHS WALK-IN CENTRE ....
Colchester 7B 6
Nicholls Way CO16: Clac S 5E 30
Nichols Cl. CO11: Law 4D 10
Nicholsons Gro. CO1: Colc 6D 42 (5C 14)
Nien-Oord CO16: Clac S 7F 31
Nightingale Cl. CO4: Colc 3J 15
CO15: Clac S 6J 31
Nightingale Ct. CO2: Colc 4D 22
Nightingale Pl. CO3: S'way 7C 12
Nightingale Way CO15: Clac S 6J 31
Noah's Ark La. CO10: Sud 4D 36
Nonsuch Mdw. CO10: Sud 5E 36
Nook, The CO7: W'hoe 4A 24
Norbury Cl. CO6: M Tey 3D 18
Norfolk Av. CO5: W Mer 4D 40
CO15: Hol S 5D 32
Norfolk Cres. CO4: Colc 2D 14
Norman Cl. CO6: M Tey 3C 18
Normandy Av. CO2: Colc 1C 22
Norman Rd. CO11: Mann 3F 11
CO15: Hol S 4C 32
Norman Way CO3: Colc 6H 13
  (Reynolds Av.)
CO3: Colc 5H 13
  (Wroxham Cl.)
Northbourne Rd. CO15: Clac S 1J 35
Northcroft CO10: Sud 4E 36
Northern App. CO4: Colc 5A 6
Northern Rd. CO10: Sud 2G 37
Northfield Gdns. CO4: Colc 6C 6
Northgate St. CO1: Colc 4A 42 (4A 14)
North Hill CO1: Colc 4A 42 (4A 14)
North La. CO6: M Tey 1F 19
North Hill Pl. CO9: Hals 2B 38
North Ri. CO10: Gt Cor 5G 37
North Rd. CO7: B'sea 5H 41
CO15: Clac S 5H 31
Nth. Sea Vw. CO12: Har 5E 26
Nth. Station Rd. CO1: Colc 1A 42 (2A 14)
North St. CO10: Sud 3E 36
CO11: Mann 3F 11
CO14: Walt 1G 29

North St. Pde. CO10: Sud 4E 36
(off North St.)
North St. Pas. CO10: Sud 4E 36
(off North St.)
North Vw. Cotts. CO6: Gt Hork 3H 5
Norway Cres. CO12: Har 4E 26
Norwich Cl. CO1: Colc 3E 42 (3C 14)
CO16: Clac S 5G 31
Norwood Av. CO15: Clac S 6A 32
Norwood Way CO14: Walt 3E 28
Nottage Cl. CO7: W'hoe 4A 24
Nottingham Rd. CO15: Hol S 5D 32
No. 1 The Maltings CO11: Mist 3H 11
Nunn's Rd. CO1: Colc 4A 42 (4A 14)
Nursery Cl. CO3: S'way 6C 12
Nursery Rd. CO10: Gt Cor 7H 37
Nuthatch Chase CO3: S'way 6B 12

O

Oakapple Cl. CO2: Colc 3K 21
Oak Av. CO16: Clac S 2D 34
Oak Cl. CO6: W Ber 6E 4
CO15: Clac S 5H 31
Oakhaven CO12: Har 6E 26
Oakland Rd. CO12: Har 4H 27
Oaklands Av. CO3: Colc 6E 12
Oakleigh Ct. CO7: W'hoe 5K 23
(off St John's Rd.)
Oakleigh Rd. CO15: Clac S 3J 31
Oakley Rd. CO12: Har 5D 26
Oak Ridge CO12: L Oak 7A 26
Oak Rd. CO5: Tip 3F 39
CO9: Hals 5A 38
CO10: Gt Cor 5H 37
Oaks, The CO13: Frin S 4D 28
Oaks Dr. CO3: Colc 4K 13
Oaks End CO2: Lay H 7G 21
Oaks Pl. CO4: Colc 7A 6
OAKS PRIVATE HOSPITAL 7A 6
Oak Tree Gdns. CO2: Colc 1E 22
Oak Tree Rd. CO7: Alr 4F 25
Oakview CO12: Har 6E 26
Oakwood Av. CO5: W Mer 4D 40
CO15: Hol S 5D 32
Oakwood Bus. Pk. CO15: Clac S 2K 31
Oakwood Cl. CO13: Kir C 4C 28
Oakwood Dr. CO5: W Mer 4D 40
Oakwood Gdns. CO5: W Mer 4D 40
Oak Yd. CO9: Hals 3B 38
Oatfield Cl. CO3: S'way 5D 12
Oatlands CO7: Elm M 5D 16
Oberon Cl. CO4: Colc 4H 15
Ocean Vw. CO14: Walt 1H 29
Ockendon Way CO14: Walt 2E 28
Odeon Cinema
Colchester 5A 42 (4A 14)
Old Chapel Dr. CO3: S'way 5D 12
Old Church La. CO6: W Ber 4D 4
Old Coach Rd. CO1: Colc 4D 14
Olde Forge CO7: B'sea 3G 41
Old Ferry Rd. CO7: W'hoe 4J 23
Old Forge Rd. CO2: Lay H 7F 21
Old Hall La. CO14: Walt 6J 29
OLD HEATH .7E 14
Old Heath Rd. CO1: Colc 6D 14
CO2: Colc 6D 14
Old House Rd. CO6: Gt Hork 2F 5
Old Ipswich Rd. CO4: L'ham 1H 7
CO7: A'lgh 4G 7
Old London Rd. CO6: M Tey 3D 18
Old Market Ct. CO10: Sud 4E 36
(off Burkitts La.)
Old Market Pl. CO10: Sud 4E 36
Old Parsonage Way CO13: Frin S 5D 28
Old Pier St. CO14: Walt 2G 29
Old Rectory Ct. CO6: M Tey 2E 18
Old Rd. CO13: Frin S 6D 28
CO15: Clac S 1H 35
Old Rose Gdn. CO4: Colc 7K 5
Old School Ct. CO7: B'sea 6G 41
(off Silcott St.)
Old School La. CO7: Elm M 5E 16
Old Vicarage Rd. CO12: Har 4G 27
Old Way CO13: Frin S 6D 28
Olive Gro. CO2: Colc 2K 21
Olivers Cl. CO15: Clac S 7H 31
Olivers Ct. CO15: Clac S 7H 31
Olivers La. CO2: Colc 5F 21
Olivers Rd. CO15: Clac S 7H 31
Olley Wlk. CO5: Tip 4J 39
Olympic Blvd. CO4: Colc 5B 6
Ongar Cl. CO16: Clac S 7E 30
Onslow Cres. CO2: Colc 4C 22

Ophir Rd. CO7: B'sea 7H 41
Orchard Av. CO9: Hals 3A 38
Orchard Cl. CO6: Cop 4H 19
CO7: Elm M 5E 16
CO16: Clac S 6F 31
Orchard Ct. CO3: Colc 4J 13
Orchard Gdns. CO4: Colc 3D 14
Orchard Lodge CO5: Tip 6H 39
(off Station Rd.)
Orchard M. CO5: Tip 6G 39
Orchard Pl. CO4: Colc 6B 6
Orchard Rd. CO1: Colc 2A 42 (3A 14)
CO7: Alr 4F 25
Orchid Fld. Ct. CO5: W Mer 5E 40
Oriel Cl. CO10: Gt Cor 5H 37
Orlando Ct. CO14: Walt 2G 29
Ormonde Cl. CO6: W Ber 6F 5
Orpen Cl. CO6: W Ber 6D 4
Orpen's Hill CO2: B'ch 7A 20
Orrin Wlk. CO4: Colc 1A 14
Orsino Wlk. CO4: Colc 4H 15
Orwell Cl. CO4: Colc 2G 15
Orwell Ho. CO12: Har 3F 27
(off Williamsburg Av.)
Orwell Rd. CO12: Har 3J 27
CO15: Clac S 2J 35
Orwell Way CO16: Clac S 6F 31
Osborne Cl. CO15: Clac S 4K 31
Osborne Cotts. CO5: Mess 1H 39
Osborne Rd. CO5: W Mer 5E 40
Osbornes Ct. CO7: B'sea 6H 41
Osborne St. CO1: Colc 6C 42 (5B 14)
Osier Cl. CO3: S'way 5D 12
Osprey Cl. CO3: S'way 7B 12
Ospreys CO15: Clac S 5J 31
Othello Cl. CO4: Colc 3H 15
Otho Dr. CO4: Colc 4C 6
Ottershaw Way CO16: Clac S 5E 30
Oulton Cl. CO12: Har 4E 26
Oulton Hall CO15: Clac S 1K 35
Outpart Eastward CO12: Har 1K 27
Owen Ward Cl. CO2: Colc 1G 21
Owls Retreat CO4: Colc 3H 15
Oxenford Cl. CO12: Har 6E 26
Oxford Cl. CO10: Gt Cor 5G 37
Oxford Ct. CO3: Colc 5K 13
Oxford Cres. CO15: Clac S 7H 31
Oxford Rd. CO3: Colc 5K 13
CO9: Hals 4A 38
CO11: Mann 3F 11
CO13: Frin S 5E 28
CO15: Clac S 1J 35
Oxley Parker Dr. CO4: Colc 4C 6
Oxton Cl. CO5: Rhdge 4J 23
Oyster Catchers, The CO7: W'hoe 5K 23
Oyster Cl. CO5: W Mer 4C 40
Oyster Pk. CO1: Colc 5F 15
Oysters Reach CO7: B'sea 6J 41
Oyster Tank Rd. CO7: B'sea 7G 41
Ozier Fld. CO9: Hals 5C 38

P

Packards La. CO6: Wmgfd 1A 4
Paddock Cl. CO12: Har 3H 27
Paddocks, The CO5: W Mer 5D 40
Paddock Way CO7: W'hoe 1A 24
Paeony Chase CO5: W Mer 3C 40
Page Rd. CO15: Clac S 1H 35
Paget Rd. CO5: Rhdge 4H 23
CO7: W'hoe 4A 24
(not continuous)
Paines Ho. CO12: Har 3F 27
(off Williamsburg Av.)
Pallant Chase CO6: Eig G 3A 12
Pallister Rd. CO15: Clac S 2J 35
Palmer Gdns. CO7: W'hoe 3K 23
Pampas Cl. CO4: Colc 6C 6
Panton Cres. CO4: Colc 4G 15
Papillon Ho. CO1: Colc 4A 42
Papillon Rd. CO3: Colc 4K 13
Parade, The CO2: Colc 3C 22
CO14: Walt 3G 29
Parade Dr. CO12: Har 6B 26
Parade Sq. CO2: Colc 7D 42 (6C 14)
Park, The CO11: Mann 3F 11
Park & Ride
Colchester 3A 6
Park Blvd. CO15: Hol S 5D 32
Park Chase CO16: St O 6A 30
Park Dr. CO5: Tip 5K 39
CO7: B'sea 5G 41
CO9: Hals 4B 38

Parker Pl. CO10: Sud 1D 36
Parker Rd. CO4: Colc 4D 6
Parker Way CO9: Hals 5B 38
Parkes Ho. CO12: Har 3F 27
(off Williamsburg Av.)
PARKESTON .2E 26
Parkeston Rd. CO12: Har 2E 26
(Princess St.)
CO12: Har 3E 26
(Sweden Cl.)
Park Farm Rd. CO6: W Ber 2D 4
Parkfield St. CO5: Rhdge 5H 23
Parkland Ct. CO1: Colc 6E 14
Parklands Ct. CO16: Clac S 1E 34
Park La. CO5: Tip 5K 39
Park Rd. CO3: Colc 5J 13
CO4: Colc 7J 15
CO7: A'lgh 7D 8
CO7: W'hoe 4A 24
CO10: Sud 3G 37
CO12: Har 3J 27
CO15: Clac S 2G 35
Parkside Quarter CO1: Colc 3A 42 (3B 14)
Park Sq. E. CO15: Jay 3C 34
Park Sq. W. CO15: Jay 3C 34
Park Ter. CO12: Har 3J 27
Park Way CO15: Clac S 3G 35
Parkwood Av. CO7: W'hoe 3K 23
Parkwood Dr. CO10: Sud 1E 36
Parmenter Dr. CO10: Gt Cor 6J 37
Parnell Cl. CO2: Colc 3C 22
Parr Cl. CO15: Jay 3C 34
Parr Dr. CO3: Colc 7E 12
Parrington Way CO11: Law 4C 10
Parry Dr. CO16: Clac S 6F 31
Parsley Ho. CO1: Colc 5A 42
Parsonage St. CO9: Hals 3C 38
Parsonon Wlk. CO4: Colc 4G 15
Parsons Ct. CO9: Hals 3C 38
(off Parsonage St.)
PARSON'S HEATH 2F 15
Parson's Heath CO4: Colc 2G 15
Parson's Hill CO3: Colc 5G 13
Parsons Hill CO7: Gt Bro 3J 17
Parsons La. CO1: Colc 5E 14
(not continuous)
Partridge La. CO3: S'way 7C 12
Paternoster Row CO14: Walt 2G 29
Pathfields Rd. CO15: Clac S 7G 31
Pathway, The CO13: Kir C 4C 28
Patmore Rd. CO4: Colc 2F 15
Patten Cl. CO6: M Tey 3D 18
Pattinson Wlk. CO6: Gt Hork 2H 5
Pattrick's La. CO12: Har 3H 27
Pauline Cl. CO15: Clac S 5A 32
Paul's Cres. CO7: Elm M 6D 16
Paul Spendlove Ct. CO4: Colc 2G 15
Pauls Way CO15: Jay 3C 34
Pavilion Vw. CO1: Colc 2C 42 (3B 14)
Paxman Av. CO2: Colc 1G 21
Paxton Rd. CO15: Clac S 3A 32
Paynters Ter. CO9: Hals 3C 38
Peacehaven CO13: Frin S 5E 28
Peace Rd. CO3: S'way 5C 12
Peache Rd. CO1: Colc 5E 14
Peakes Cl. CO5: Tip 6F 39
Pearce Ct. CO2: Colc 7B 42 (6B 14)
Pearl Wlk. CO7: W'hoe 5A 24
Pearmain Way CO3: S'way 7C 12
Peartree Bus. Cen. CO3: S'way 7E 12
Pear Tree Cl. CO9: Hals 2D 38
Pear Tree Ct. CO5: Tip 6H 39
Peartree Rd. CO3: S'way 7D 12
Peartree Way CO16: L Cla 1F 31
Peawood La. CO7: A'lgh 2C 8
Pebmarsh Cl. CO2: Colc 4C 22
Pecockes Cl. CO10: Gt Cor 6J 37
Pedder's Cl. CO3: Colc 1F 21
Peerswood Rd. CO2: Colc 2K 21
Pegasus Way CO4: Colc 2E 14
Pelham Cl. CO12: Har 5E 26
Pelhams La. CO1: Colc 5B 42 (4B 14)
Pembroke Cl. CO2: Colc 1E 22
Pembroke Gdns. CO15: Hol S 5D 32
Pembroke Pl. CO10: Sud 1D 36
Penfold Rd. CO15: Clac S 2H 35
Pennsylvania La. CO5: Tip 4F 39
(not continuous)
Penrice Cl. CO4: Colc 5G 15
Penzance Cl. CO15: Clac S 4F 35
Peppercorn Cl. CO4: Colc 1B 14
Pepper's Rd. CO4: Boxt 1A 6
Pepys Ho. CO12: Har 3F 27
(off Williamsburg Av.)
Pepys St. CO12: Har 2J 27

Percival Rd. CO13: Kir S 1B 28
  CO14: Walt .7H 29
Percy Ruse Cl. CO10: Sud 4H 37
Peregrine Cl. CO15: Clac S 4J 31
Peregrine Ct. CO4: Colc 3H 15
Perryfields CO10: Gt Cor 7H 37
Perry Rd. CO5: Tip 5F 39
Persardi Ct. CO2: Colc 5C 22
Pershore End CO3: Colc 6E 12
Perth Cl. CO2: Colc 3C 22
Pertwee Cl. CO7: B'sea 4G 41
Pertwees Ct. CO1: Colc 5E 14
Peter Bruff Av. CO16: Clac S 6F 31
Peto Av. CO4: Colc 1B 14
Petrel Ho. CO12: Har 3H 27
Petrolea Cl. CO4: Colc 2A 14
Petronius Way CO4: Colc 5D 6
Petworth Cl. CO7: W'hoe 4A 24
Pevensey Dr. CO15: Clac S 4F 35
Pharos La. CO5: W Mer 5C 40
Pheonix Cl. CO10: Sud 3E 36
Philbrick Cl. CO1: Colc 6E 14
Philip Cl. CO14: Walt 2E 28
Phillip Rd. CO7: W'hoe 4K 23
Phillips Fld. Rd. CO10: Gt Cor 6G 37
Phoenix Cl. CO5: W Mer 5B 40
Phoenix Ct. CO2: Colc 6F 15
Phoenix Ind. Pk. CO12: Har 2F 27
Phoenix Pavilions CO12: Har 5H 27
Phoenix Sq. CO4: Colc 5E 6
Pickers Way CO15: Hol S 4D 32
Pickford Wlk. CO4: Colc 4H 15
Pier App. CO14: Walt 3G 29
Pier Av. CO15: Clac S 1H 35
Pierce Glade CO5: Tip 5G 39
Pier Cl. CO2: Colc 3B 22
Pier Gap CO15: Clac S 2J 35
Pightle Way CO14: Walt 3E 28
Pilborough Way CO3: Colc 1E 20
Pill Box Wlk. CO1: Colc 1E 42 (2C 14)
Pinecroft Gdns. CO4: Colc 7D 6
Pinecroft Ri. CO10: Ball 6C 36
Pine Gro. CO5: W Mer 4B 40
Pines, The CO10: Sud 2G 37
Pine Tree Ct. CO4: Colc 2G 15
Pinewood Cl. CO13: Kir C 4B 28
  CO15: Clac S 4H 31
Pioneer Pl. CO1: Colc 7D 42
Piper Rd. CO3: Colc 4H 13
Pippins, The CO4: Colc 3E 14
  CO9: Hals .3A 38
Pirie Rd. CO6: W Ber 6E 4
Pit La. CO5: Tip .4G 39
Place Farm Ct. CO2: Colc 2F 23
Plains Farm Cl. CO7: A'lgh, Colc 4F 7
Plane Vw. Cl. CO16: Clac S 2E 34
Planton Way CO7: B'sea 5F 41
Playford Ct. CO10: Sud 3E 36
                   (off Inkerman Row)
Pleasant M. CO5: W Mer 5C 40
Pleasant Plains M. CO5: W Mer 4K 5
Plough Dr. CO3: Colc 6G 13
Plough La. CO10: Sud 4D 36
Ploughman's Headland CO3: S'way 6D 12
Plover Cl. CO13: Kir C 4C 28
Plover Rd. CO3: S'way 6B 12
Plowright Ho. CO1: Colc 3A 42
Plume Av. CO3: Colc 7G 13
Plymouth Rd. CO15: Clac S 4G 35
Podium Cl. CO4: Colc 4C 6
Point, The CO4: Colc 3D 6
POINT CLEAR 7H 41
Pole Barn La. CO13: Frin S 5D 28
Pollard Wlk. CO16: Clac S 6F 31
Polley Cl. CO13: Kir C 3C 28
Polstead Way CO16: Clac S 7E 30
Pond Chase CO3: Colc 7G 13
Pondfield Rd. CO4: Colc 2F 15
Pond Ho. La. CO15: Clac S 3C 32
Pondtail Ct. CO13: Kir C 4A 28
Pope's La. CO3: Colc 4A 14
Poplar Av. CO16: Clac S 2D 34
Poplar Cl. CO9: Hals 5C 38
  CO15: Clac S 2E 34
Poplar Ct. CO10: Gt Cor 4H 37
Poplar Hall Cl. CO1: Colc 1A 42 (2A 14)
Poplar Rd. CO10: Gt Cor 4H 37
Poplars, The CO3: Colc 6E 12
Poplars Cl. CO7: Alr 5F 25
Poplar Way CO13: Kir C 4B 28
Poppy Gdns. CO2: Colc 1E 22
Portal Pct. CO1: Colc 5B 42 (4H 14)
Porters Brook Wlk. CO4: Colc 1E 14
PORTERS GREEN 7F 19
Porter Way CO16: Clac S 7E 30

Portland Av. CO12: Har 4H 27
Portland Cres. CO12: Har 4H 27
Portland Rd. CO2: Colc 6C 42 (5B 14)
Port La. CO1: Colc 5D 14
Portlight Cl. CO11: Mist 3J 11
Portobello Rd. CO14: Walt 2G 29
Portsmouth Rd. CO15: Clac S 4G 35
Portway Ct. CO9: Hals 2C 38
Posford Ct. CO4: Colc 5B 6
Pot Kiln Rd. CO10: Gt Cor 6H 37
Pot Kilns, The CO10: Gt Cor 5J 37
Potter Cl. CO4: Colc 6D 30
Potter M. CO4: Colc 1B 14
Pottersfield CO10: Gt Cor 7H 37
POTTS GREEN .4D 18
Pound Farm Dr. CO12: Har 4E 26
Poundfield Cl. CO7: Alr 5F 25
Powell Cl. CO5: Tip 5J 39
  CO16: Clac S 6E 30
Pownall Cres. CO2: Colc 7B 14
Poynter Pl. CO13: Kir C 3C 28
President Rd. CO3: Colc 6E 12
Preston Rd. CO15: Hol S 6C 32
Pretoria Rd. CO9: Hals 3C 38
Prettygate Rd. CO3: Colc 6G 13
                 (not continuous)
Primrose La. CO5: Tip 4G 39
Primrose Rd. CO15: Hol S 5D 32
Primrose Wlk. CO4: Colc 3G 15
Primula Cl. CO16: Clac S 7F 31
Prince Albert Rd. CO5: W Mer 5D 40
Prince Charles Cl. CO10: Sud 3F 37
  CO15: Clac S 3F 35
Prince Charles Rd. CO2: Colc 2C 22
PRINCE OF WALES RDBT. 2F 19
Prince Philip Av. CO15: Clac S 3F 35
Prince Philip Rd. CO2: Colc 3B 22
Prince's Esplanade CO14: Walt 2H 29
Princes Rd. CO12: Har 4G 27
  CO15: Hol S 5C 32
Princess Anne Cl. CO15: Clac S 3F 35
Princess Dr. CO4: Colc 5E 6
Princess St. CO12: Har 2E 26
Princes Theatre
  Clacton-on-Sea 1J 35
               (off Station Rd.)
Prince St. CO10: Sud 3E 36
Princeton M. CO4: Colc 6D 6
Prior Cl. CO9: Hals 5A 38
Prior Way CO4: Colc 1K 13
Priory Ct. CO3: Colc 5A 14
Priory Gdns. CO10: Sud 5E 36
Priory Rd. CO10: Sud 2D 36
  CO15: Clac S 1H 35
Priory St. CO1: Colc 5C 42 (4B 14)
Priory Wlk. CO1: Colc 5C 42 (4B 14)
  CO10: Sud 5E 36
Proctor Way CO6: M Tey 3C 18
Progress Way CO16: L Cla 2F 31
Promenade CO12: Har 6G 27
  CO15: Clac S, Jay 5E 34
  CO15: Hol S 7A 32
  CO16: St O 6A 34
Promenade Way CO7: B'sea 7F 41
Propelair Way CO4: Colc 1K 13
Prospect Hill CO10: Gt Cor, L Cor 7K 37
Prospect Pl. CO9: Hals 4B 38
Prospero Cl. CO4: Colc 4H 15
Provence Cl. CO3: S'way 4C 12
Providence Rd. CO1: Colc 5D 14
Prunus Ct. CO2: Colc 5C 22
Puffinsdale CO15: Clac S 6J 31
Pulpitfield Cl. CO14: Walt 2E 28
Pump Hill CO16: St O 7A 30
Purbeck Ct. CO1: Colc 4F 15
                (off Tabor Rd.)
Purcell Cl. CO4: Colc 5E 15
Purley Way CO16: Clac S 5E 30
Purvis Way CO4: Colc 5D 6
Pyefleet Cl. CO5: Fing 6A 24
  CO7: B'sea .5G 41
Pyefleet Ho. CO5: W Mer 4D 40
           (off Carrington Ct.)
Pyesand CO13: Kir S 2A 28

Q

Quakers All. CO1: Colc 4B 42 (4B 14)
Quay, The CO7: W'hoe 5K 23
  CO12: Har .1J 27
Quay Courtyard CO11: Mann 3F 11
Quay La. CO10: Sud 5E 36
  CO13: Kir S 1B 28
Quayside Dr. CO2: Colc 6F 15

Quayside Maltings, The CO11: Mist 3H 11
Quay St. CO7: W'hoe 4K 23
  CO11: Mann 3F 11
Quay Theatre, The 5E 36
Queen Anne Dr. CO5: W Mer 5D 40
Queen Anne Gdns. CO5: W Mer 5D 40
Queen Anne Rd. CO5: W Mer 5D 40
Queen Elizabeth Av. CO15: Clac S 3F 35
Queen Elizabeth Way CO2: Colc 3C 22
Queen Mary Av. CO2: Colc 7B 14
Queensberry Av. CO6: Cop 2H 19
Queensbury Cl. CO5: W Mer 5E 40
Queens Cl. CO10: Gt Cor 6H 37
  CO10: Sud 3E 36
Queens Cnr. CO5: W Mer 4D 40
Queen's Ct. CO15: Hol S 7C 32
Queens Ct. CO5: W Mer 4D 40
                   (off East Rd.)
Queen's Ho. CO13: Frin S 6D 28
Queensland Dr. CO2: Colc 3C 22
Queens M. CO5: W Mer 5B 40
Queen's Rd. CO3: Colc 5J 13
  CO6: W Ber 7D 4
  CO7: W'hoe 4K 23
  CO12: Har .5F 27
  CO13: Frin S 6D 28
  CO15: Clac S 3G 35
Queens Rd. CO10: Sud 2E 36
Queen St. CO1: Colc 5C 42 (4B 14)
  CO7: B'sea .6H 41
Queensway CO15: Tip 4G 39
  CO10: Gt Cor 6H 37
  CO11: Law 3E 10
  CO15: Hol S 6C 32
Quendon Way CO13: Frin S 4E 28
Quilters Cl. CO15: Hol S 5E 32
Quince Ct. CO5: Tip 6J 39

R

Radiator Rd. CO10: Gt Cor 6G 37
Radvald Chase CO3: S'way 7E 12
Raeburn Cl. CO13: Kir C 3D 28
Raglan M. CO15: Clac S 1F 35
Raglan Rd. CO13: Frin S 5E 28
Railway St. CO11: Mann 3F 11
Railway Ter. CO15: Clac S 1J 35
Rainbow Rd. CO5: W Mer 5D 40
Rainham Way CO13: Frin S 4F 29
Rainsborowe Rd. CO2: Colc 7J 13
Raleigh Cl. CO10: Sud 1G 37
Raleigh Rd. CO10: Sud 1G 37
Rambler Cl. CO3: S'way 4H 5
Ram Kuteer Dr. CO6: Gt Hork 4H 5
Ramparts Cl. CO6: Gt Hork 3H 5
Ramparts Cotts. CO6: Gt Hork 3H 5
Ramparts Ct. CO4: Colc 7H 5
Ramplings Av. CO15: Clac S 6H 31
Ramsden Cl. CO15: Clac S 6K 31
RAMSEY 5A 26
Ramsey M. CO2: Colc 7C 14
Ramsey Rd. CO9: Hals 4A 38
  CO12: Har, R'sy 6A 26
Ranger Wlk. CO2: Colc 1D 22
Range Vw. CO4: Colc 1E 22
Rangoon Cl. CO2: Colc 3H 21
Ransom Rd. CO5: Tip 5G 39
Ratcliffe Cl. CO4: Colc 3D 14
Ratcliffe Rd. CO3: Colc 5E 12
Raven's Av. CO9: Hals 4C 38
Ravensdale CO15: Clac S 3A 34
Ravenswood CO1: Colc 7E 42 (5D 14)
Raven Way CO4: Colc 6A 6
Rawden Cl. CO12: Har 3G 27
Rawlings Cres. CO4: Colc 5D 6
Rawstorn Rd. CO3: Colc 4A 14
Ray Av. CO12: Har 3F 27
Raycliff Av. CO15: Clac S 5H 31
Raydon Way CO10: Gt Cor 5J 37
Rayhaven CO12: R'sy 5B 26
Ray Ho. CO5: W Mer 4D 40
           (off Carrington Ct.)
Ray Island (Nature Reserve) 2A 40
Ray La. CO12: Har, R'sy 4A 26
Rayleigh Cl. CO4: Colc 2D 14
Rayleigh Mans. CO2: Colc 6J 13
Raymouth Rd. CO2: Colc 2A 22
Rayner Rd. CO2: Colc 1H 21
Rayner Way CO9: Hals 4B 38
Reaper Rd. CO3: Colc 7G 13
Rebow Rd. CO7: W'hoe 4K 23
  CO12: Har .5F 27
Rebow St. CO1: Colc 5D 14
Reckitts Cl. CO15: Clac S 7A 32

Recreation Rd. CO1: Colc 6D 14
   CO15: Clac S 1J 35
Recreation Wlk.
   CO10: Gt Cor 6H 37
Recreation Way CO7: B'sea 5H 41
Rectory Cl. CO4: Colc 1A 14
Rectory Hill CO7: W'hoe 3A 24
Rectory La. CO12: L Oak, R'sy 6A 26, 7A 26
   (not continuous)
Rectory Rd. CO5: Rhdge 4G 23
   CO5: Tip 5G 39
   CO6: Cop 5G 19
   CO7: Frat 3J 25
   CO7: W'hoe 2A 24
   CO10: Midd 7E 36
   CO12: L Oak 7A 26
   CO16: Wee H 2B 30
Red Barn Cl. CO7: B'sea 4H 41
Red Barn Rd. CO7: B'sea 4H 41
Redbridge Rd. CO15: Clac S 3J 31
Reddells Cl. CO10: Sud 3F 37
Rede Way CO10: Gt Cor 5J 37
Red Ho. La. CO10: Gt Cor 7G 37
   CO10: Sud 4E 36
Redhouse La. CO4: Boxt 1K 5
Red Lion Yd. CO1: Colc 5B 42 (4B 14)
Redmill CO3: Colc 1G 21
Redrose Wlk. CO16: Clac S 7F 31
Redwood Cl. CO4: Colc 2G 15
Redwood Ct. CO4: Colc 3G 15
Reed Cl. CO16: Clac S 6F 31
Reed Hall Av. CO2: Colc 1J 21
Reed Wlk. CO1: Colc 1E 42 (2C 14)
Refinery Rd. CO12: Har 2C 26
Regency Ct. CO2: Colc 7E 14
Regency Grn. CO3: Colc 7F 13
Regency Lodge CO15: Clac S 6H 31
Regent Cl. CO7: B'sea 4H 41
Regent Rd. CO7: B'sea 5H 41
Regents Cl. CO4: Colc 5E 6
Regent St. CO5: Rhdge 4H 23
   CO11: Mann 3F 11
Regimental Way CO12: Har 6B 26
Reigate Av. CO16: Clac S 5G 31
Rembrandt Way CO3: Colc 6H 13
Remercie Rd. CO11: Mist 3J 11
Remus Cl. CO4: Colc 5B 6
Retreat, The CO6: W Ber 7D 4
Reverdy Ho. CO2: Colc 2A 22
Reymead Cl. CO5: W Mer 5C 40
Reynard Hgts. CO4: Colc 3E 14
Reynards Cl. CO13: Kir C 4B 28
Reynards Copse CO4: Colc 7C 6
Reynolds Av. CO3: Colc 6H 13
Reynolds Way CO10: Sud 1G 37
Richard Av. CO7: B'sea 6H 41
   CO7: W'hoe 1A 24
Richard Burn Way CO10: Sud 1E 36
Richard Day Wlk. CO2: Colc 3B 22
Richardson Wlk. CO3: Colc 6F 13
Richards Wlk. CO15: Clac S 5H 31
Richmond Cres. CO12: Har 5G 27
Richmond Dr. CO15: Jay 3D 34
Richmond Rd. CO2: Colc 7A 14
   CO5: W Mer 5D 40
Riddles Dr. CO4: Colc 1B 14
Ridge, The CO14: Walt 2F 29
Ridgeway CO4: Colc 6C 6
Ridgeway, The CO12: Har 4F 27
Ridgewell Way CO2: Colc 3B 22
Rigby Av. CO11: Mist 4J 11
Rigby Rd. CO11: Mist 3H 11
Rigdon's La. CO14: Walt 1D 28
Riley Av. CO15: Jay 6B 34
Rimini Cl. CO2: Colc 1J 21
Rimmer Cl. CO10: Sud 1G 37
Riparian Sq. CO1: Colc 1E 42 (2C 14)
Ripley Cl. CO16: Clac S 5E 30
Ripple Way CO4: Colc 2D 14
Risby Cl. CO16: Clac S 7D 30
Rise, The CO6: Eig G 3C 8
River Bank Wlk. CO1: Colc 1E 42 (3C 14)
River Cl. CO9: Hals 4C 38
Riverside Av. E. CO11: Law 2E 10
Riverside Av. W. CO11: Law 2E 10
Riverside Ct. CO9: Hals *3B 38*
   (off Rosemary La.)
Riverside Pl. CO1: Colc 3D 14
Riverside Wlk. CO1: Colc 3A 42 (3A 14)
Riverview CO11: Law 3E 10
Roach Va. CO4: Colc 2G 15
Robertson Cl. CO15: Clac S 2G 35
Roberts Rd. CO2: Colc 6C 14
Robert Way CO7: W'hoe 1A 24
Robin Cres. CO3: S'way 7B 12

Robinia Ct. CO4: Colc *4G 15*
   (off Blackthorn Av.)
Robinsdale CO15: Clac S 5J 31
Robinson Rd. CO7: B'sea 5J 41
Robin Way CO10: Ball 6C 36
Rochdale Way CO4: Colc 5G 15
Rochester Way CO10: Sud 1D 36
Rochford Way CO13: Frin S 3D 28
   CO14: Walt 2E 28
Rockhampton Wlk. CO2: Colc 3C 22
Rockingham Cl. CO4: Colc 7F 7
Rodney Cl. CO3: Colc 5J 13
Rogation Cl. CO3: S'way 5D 12
Roger Browning Ho. CO1: Colc 4C 42
Rokell Way CO13: Kir C 4C 28
Rollerworld
   Colchester 4D 14
Roman Cir. Way CO2: Colc 7A 42 (5A 14)
Roman Hill CO2: Colc 5D 22
Roman River Valley Nature Reserve 6F 21
Roman Rd. CO1: Colc 3D 42 (3C 14)
Roman Way CO2: Colc 1A 22
Romford Cl. CO4: Colc 2D 14
Romney Cl. CO7: B'sea 3G 41
   CO13: Kir C 3C 28
   CO16: Clac S 6G 31
Romulus Cl. CO4: Colc 5B 6
Ronald Rd. CO9: Hals 5B 38
Rookeries, The CO6: M Tey 2G 19
Rookery, The CO11: Law 3E 10
Rookery Chase CO7: A'lgh 1B 8
Rookery La. CO5: Tip 3G 39
Rookwood Cl. CO15: Clac S 4G 31
Roosevelt Way CO2: Colc 7D 14
Roper Cl. CO4: Colc 4D 6
Rope Wlk. CO7: B'sea 6J 41
Rosabelle Av. CO7: W'hoe 3K 23
Rosalind Cl. CO4: Colc 4H 15
Rose Allen Av. CO2: Colc 4B 22
Rose Av. CO3: S'way 7C 12
Rosebank CO12: Har 4F 27
Rosebank Rd. CO5: W Mer 5B 40
Rosebery Av. CO1: Colc 5E 42 (4C 14)
Rose Ct. CO2: Colc 4D 22
Rose Cres. CO4: Colc 1K 13
   CO15: Clac S 4J 31
Rosecroft Cl. CO15: Clac S 5H 31
Rosedale Cotts. CO3: S'way 1K 19
Rose Ho. CO1: Colc 7E 42
Rosemary Av. CO7: W'hoe 5K 23
Rosemary Almshouses CO3: S'way 1K 19
Rosemary Cl. CO5: Tip 5G 39
Rosemary Ct. CO4: Colc 3G 15
Rosemary Cres. CO5: Tip 5G 39
   CO15: Clac S 2J 35
Rosemary Gdns. CO10: Sud 1F 37
Rosemary La. CO9: Hals 3B 38
Rosemary Rd. CO15: Clac S 2H 35
Rosemary Rd. W. CO15: Clac S 2H 35
Rosemary Way CO15: Jay 5D 34
Rosetta Cl. CO7: W'hoe 2K 23
Rosewood Cl. CO4: Colc 6C 6
Rosewood Pk. CO11: Mist 4J 11
Rossendale Cl. CO4: Colc 7F 7
Rotary Way CO3: Colc 3A 14
Roundacre CO9: Hals 5B 38
Round Cl. CO3: Colc 4H 13
Rouses La. CO16: Clac S 7C 30
Rouse Way CO1: Colc 4D 14
Rouses Way CO15: Jay 5B 34
Rowallan Cl. CO3: Colc 1G 21
Rowan Chase CO5: Tip 4G 39
Rowan Cl. CO3: S'way 7D 12
   CO12: Har 4G 27
   CO15: Clac S 1F 35
Rowan Pl. CO1: Colc 1A 42 (2A 14)
Rowhedge Bus. Pk. CO5: Rhdge 4G 23
Rowhedge Rd. CO2: Colc 2F 23
   CO5: Rhdge 2F 23
Rowland's Yd. CO12: Har 5D 26
Roxborough Cl. CO6: M Tey 3C 18
Royal Ct. CO4: Colc 2G 15
Roydon Way CO13: Frin S 4D 28
Ruaton Dr. CO16: Clac S 7F 31
Rubens Wlk. CO10: Sud 1G 37
Rudd Ct. CO4: Colc 1F 15
Rudkin Rd. CO4: Colc 5B 6
Rudsdale Way CO3: Colc 6F 13
Rugby Rd. CO10: Gt Cor 7H 37
Rugosa Cl. CO3: S'way 4C 12
Rush Grn. Rd. CO16: Clac S 2D 34
Rushmere Cl. CO5: W Mer 5D 40
Ruskin Cl. CO13: Kir C 3C 28

Russell Ct. CO2: Colc *7D 14*
   (off Stalin Rd.)
Russell Rd. CO15: Clac S 1K 35
Rutland Av. CO2: Colc 1H 21
Ryde Av. CO15: Clac S 3K 31
Rye Cl. CO3: S'way 6E 12
   CO7: B'sea 3G 41
Ryegate Rd. CO1: Colc 3C 42 (4B 14)
Rye Hill CO10: Sud 4H 37
Rye Hills CO9: Hals 5C 38
Rye La. CO2: Lay H 7G 21

S

Sacketts Gro. Cvn. Pk. CO16: Clac S 2C 34
Sackville Way CO6: W Ber 6D 4
Saddle M. CO3: S'way 5D 12
Sadler Cl. CO2: Colc 7D 14
Sadlers Cl. CO13: Kir C 4A 28
Saffron Way CO5: Tip 6G 39
Sage Rd. CO2: Colc 2C 22
Sage Wlk. CO5: Tip 6G 39
St Alban's Rd. CO3: Colc 4K 13
St Albans Rd. CO15: Clac S 1K 35
St Albright Cres. CO3: S'way 5D 12
St Andrew's Av. CO4: Colc 3E 14
   (not continuous)
St Andrews Cl. CO7: Alr 5F 25
St Andrews Gdns. CO4: Colc 3E 14
St Andrews Pl. CO7: B'sea 3G 41
St Andrew's Rd. CO15: Clac S 1H 35
St Andrews Rd. CO9: Hals 3C 38
   CO10: Gt Cor 5G 37
St Annes Rd. CO4: Colc 3E 14
St Annes Ct. CO4: Colc 7H 31
   CO15: Clac S 7H 31
St Augustine M. CO1: Colc ...5E 42 (4C 14)
St Austell Rd. CO4: Colc 1F 15
St Austin's La. CO12: Har 1J 27
St Barbara's Rd. CO2: Colc 7K 13
St Bartholomew Cl. CO4: Colc 7E 6
St Bartholomews La. CO10: Sud 2D 36
St Benedicts Cl. CO10: Sud 1D 36
St Bernard Rd. CO4: Colc 1F 15
St Botolph's Chu. Wlk. CO2: Colc ..6C 42 (5B 14)
St Botolph's Cir. CO2: Colc ..6C 42 (5B 14)
St Botolphs Priory 6C 42 (5C 14)
St Botolph's St. CO2: Colc ...6C 42 (5B 14)
St Botolph's Ter. CO14: Walt 2G 29
St Brelades Cl. CO15: Clac S 6A 32
St Bride Ct. CO4: Colc 1F 15
St Catherines Cl. CO2: Colc 3K 21
St Christopher Rd. CO4: Colc 1F 15
St Christophers Way CO15: Jay 5D 34
St Clair Cl. CO15: Clac S 3J 31
St Clare Dr. CO3: Colc 4G 13
St Clare Rd. CO3: Colc 5G 13
St Clement Rd. CO4: Colc 1F 15
St Clements Cl. CO16: Clac S 6F 31
St Columb Ct. CO4: Colc 1E 14
St Cyrus Rd. CO4: Colc 1F 15
St Davids Cl. CO4: Colc 4E 14
St Denis Cl. CO12: Har 6F 27
St Dominic Rd. CO4: Colc 1F 15
St Edmunds Cl. CO12: Har 6F 27
St Edmund's Ct. CO4: Colc 3E 14
St Edmunds Ho. *CO4: Colc* *3G 15*
   (off Tamarisk Way)
St Faith Rd. CO4: Colc 1F 15
St Ferndale Rd. CO12: Har 2J 27
St Fillan Rd. CO4: Colc 1F 15
St George's Av. CO12: Har 5H 27
St Georges Cl. CO7: Gt Bro 2J 17
St Gregorys Ct. CO10: Sud 3D 36
ST HELENA HOSPICE
   Clacton 2H 35
   Colchester 7D 6
St Helena M. CO3: Colc 6K 13
St Helena Rd. CO3: Colc 6K 13
St Helens Av. CO15: Clac S 3K 31
St Helen's Grn. CO12: Har 2K 27
St Helens La. CO1: Colc 4B 42 (4B 14)
St Helier Cl. CO15: Clac S 7A 32
St Ives Cl. CO16: Clac S 1E 34
St James Cl. CO9: Hals 5B 38
St James Ct. CO1: Colc 4E 42
   CO7: B'sea 3G 41
St James's Ri. CO1: Colc 5D 42 (4C 14)
St Jean Wlk. CO5: Tip 4H 39
St John's Abbey Gate 7B 42 (5B 14)
St John's Av. CO2: Colc 6B 42 (5B 14)
St John's Cl. CO4: Colc 6F 7
St Johns Cres. CO6: Gt Hork 3H 5
St John's Gdns. CO15: Clac S 5H 31
St John's Grn. CO2: Colc 6B 42 (5B 14)

St John's Pl. CO2: Colc 6B 42
St John's Rd. CO4: Colc 7F 7
  CO7: W'hoe 5A 24
  CO15: Clac S 6H 31
  CO16: Clac S 7A 30
St John's St. CO2: Colc 6A 42 (5A 14)
St John's Wlk. CO2: Colc 6B 42 (5B 14)
St John's Wynd CO1: Colc 6B 42 (5A 14)
St Joseph Rd. CO4: Colc 7E 6
St Jude Cl. CO4: Colc 1F 15
St Jude Gdns. CO4: Colc 1G 15
St Julian Gro. CO1: Colc 6D 42 (5C 14)
St Lawrence Rd. CO4: Colc 1F 15
St Leonard's Rd. CO1: Colc 5E 14
St Leonards Ter. CO1: Colc 5E 14
  (off St Leonard's Rd)
St Luke's Chase CO5: Tip 6H 39
St Luke's Cl. CO4: Colc 1F 15
St Mark Dr. CO4: Colc 1F 15
St Marks Rd. CO15: Clac S 7H 31
St Martins Cl. CO15: Clac S 7H 31
St Mary's Cl. CO10: Sud 1H 37
St Mary's Ct. CO15: Clac S 1H 35
St Marys Flds. CO3: Colc 4A 42 (4A 14)
St Mary's Rd. CO13: Frin S 5E 28
  CO15: Clac S 7H 31
St Michael's Chase CO6: Cop 4H 10
St Michaels Ct. CO11: Mann 3F 11
St Michael's Rd. CO12: Har 5G 27
St Michaels Rd. CO12: Har 3J 21
St Monance Way CO4: Colc 1F 15
St Neots Cl. CO4: Colc 1F 15
St Nicholas Ho. CO12: Har 3F 27
  (off Williamsburg Av.)
St Nicholas Pas. CO1: Colc 5B 42 (4B 14)
St Nicholas St. CO1: Colc 5C 42 (4B 14)
St Osyth Beach Holiday Pk. CO16: St O 6A 34
ST OSYTH HEATH 1A 30
St Osyth Rd. CO7: Alr 6H 25
  CO15: Clac S 1F 35
  CO16: L Cla, Wee H 3E 30
St Osyth Rd. E. CO16: L Cla 2F 31
St Osyth Rd. W. CO16: L Cla 2E 30
St Paul's Rd. CO1: Colc 2A 42 (3A 14)
  CO15: Clac S 1K 35
St Peter's Ct. CO1: Colc 3A 42
St Peters Ct. CO10: Sud 4E 36
  (off Christopher La.)
St Peter's Rd. CO5: W Mer 5B 40
St Peter's St. CO1: Colc 3A 42 (3A 14)
St Peter's Yd. CO1: Colc 3A 42
St Runwald St. CO1: Colc 4B 42 (4B 14)
St Saviour Cl. CO4: Colc 1F 15
St Thomas Cl. CO4: Colc 1G 15
St Vincent Rd. CO15: Clac S 3G 35
Sainty Cl. CO7: W'hoe 4A 24
Salamanca Way CO2: Colc 2J 21
Salary Cl. CO4: Colc 2G 15
Salerno Cres. CO2: Colc 2J 21
Salisbury Av. CO3: Colc 5A 14
Salisbury Cl. CO15: Hol S 6D 32
Salisbury Rd. CO15: Hol S 6B 32
Salisbury Ter. CO10: Sud 3E 36
  (off Gainsborough Rd.)
Salis Cl. CO5: Tip 7G 39
Salmon Cl. CO3: Colc 7F 13
  CO16: Clac S 6D 30
Salter Ct. CO3: Colc 4A 42
Salter Hall M. CO10: Sud 4D 36
  (off Plough La.)
Saltings Cres. CO5: W Mer 4E 40
Salvia Cl. CO3: Colc 7F 31
Sampson's La. CO5: Pel 1A 40
Samsons Cl. CO7: B'sea 4G 41
Samson's Rd. CO7: B'sea 3G 41
Sanders Dr. CO3: Colc 4H 13
Sanderson M. CO1: Colc 4B 42
  CO5: Rhdge 4H 23
Sandford Cl. CO7: W'hoe 4A 24
Sandmartin Cres. CO3: S'way 7C 12
Sandon Cl. CO6: Gt Hork 3J 5
Sandown Cl. CO15: Clac S 3K 31
Sandpiper Cl. CO4: Colc 3J 15
Sandra Ct. CO2: Colc 6A 42
Sandringham Ct. CO10: Sud 4G 37
Sandringham Dr. CO2: Colc 7C 14
Sandwich Rd. CO7: B'sea 4H 41
  CO15: Clac S 4F 35
Sandy La. CO10: Ball, Bulm 6A 36
Saran Ct. CO7: W'hoe 2J 23
Sargeant Cl. CO2: Colc 1D 22
Sarre Way CO7: B'sea 4G 41
Saville St. CO14: Walt 1G 29
Savill Rd. CO2: Colc 2E 22
Saw Mill Rd. CO1: Colc 5D 14

Saxmundham Way CO16: Clac S 7D 30
Saxon Cl. CO3: Colc 7F 13
  CO9: Hals 3C 38
Saxon Way CO15: Hol S 5E 32
Saxstead Dr. CO16: Clac S 7D 30
Scarfe Way CO4: Colc 5G 15
Scarletts Chase CO6: Gt Hork, W Ber 4E 4
Scarletts Rd. CO1: Colc 6E 14
Scheregate CO2: Colc 6B 42 (4B 14)
Schofield Cl. CO16: Clac S 6D 30
School Chase CO9: Hals 5B 38
School Ct. CO12: Har 3J 27
School Hill CO2: B'ch 6A 20
School Ho. CO1: Colc 7E 42
School La. CO6: Gt Hork 1F 5
  CO6: W Ber 6E 4
  CO7: Frat 4K 25
  CO11: Law 5C 10
  CO11: Mist 3H 11
School Rd. CO2: Colc 2C 22
  CO5: Mess 1G 39
  CO6: Cop 2H 19
  CO7: Elm M 1D 24
  CO13: Frin S 5C 28
School St. CO10: Sud 4E 36
Scofield Ct. CO10: Gt Cor 5G 37
Scott Dr. CO3: Colc 5F 13
Scrivener Cl. CO4: Colc 4C 6
Scythe Way CO3: Colc 7F 13
Sea Cornflower Way CO15: Jay 5D 34
Sea Cres. CO15: Jay 6C 34
Seaden Ct. CO15: Clac S 2A 32
Seafield Av. CO11: Mist 3K 11
Seafield Rd. CO12: Har 5G 27
Seafields Gdns. CO15: Clac S 6B 32
Seafields Rd. CO15: Clac S, Hol S 6B 32
Sea Flowers Way CO15: Jay 5D 34
Sea Glebe Way CO15: Jay 5D 34
Sea Holly Way CO15: Jay 6D 34
Sea King Cres. CO4: Colc 6D 6
Sea La. CO15: Clac S, Hol S 6B 32
Sea Lavender Way CO15: Jay 5D 34
Sea Pink Way CO15: Jay 6D 34
Seaquarium
  Clacton-on-Sea 3J 35
Searle Way CO6: Eig G 2B 12
Sea Rosemary Way CO15: Jay 5D 34
Sea Shell Way CO15: Jay 6D 34
Sea Thistle Way CO15: Jay 6D 34
Seaton Cl. CO11: Law 4D 10
Seaview Av. CO5: W Mer 4E 40
  CO12: L Oak 7B 26
Seaview Gdns. CO7: B'sea 5H 41
Seaview Hgts. CO14: Walt 3G 29
Seaview Rd. CO7: B'sea 5H 41
Sea Way CO15: Jay 6C 34
SEAWICK 5A 34
Sebastian Cl. CO4: Colc 4G 15
Second Av. CO9: Hals 4E 38
  CO10: Sud 2F 37
  CO12: Har 4H 27
  CO13: Frin S 6C 28
  CO14: Walt 6J 29
  CO15: Clac S 7A 32
Secundus Dr. CO2: Colc 1B 22
Seedbed Cen. CO4: Colc 4E 6
Seedfield, The CO5: W Mer 5B 40
Selby Cl. CO2: Colc 3K 21
Seldon Rd. CO5: Tip 5H 39
Selhurst Ct. CO14: Walt 3D 28
Selsey Av. CO15: Clac S 4F 35
Serpentine Wlk. CO1: Colc 2A 42 (3A 14)
Severalls Ind Est. CO4: Colc 5E 6
Severalls La. CO4: Boxt, Colc 2C 6
Severalls La. Cvn. Pk. CO4: Colc 3D 6
Severn Rd. CO15: Clac S 6J 31
Sewell Ho. CO7: B'sea 7G 41
Sexton Cl. CO4: Colc 4D 22
Seymour Rd. CO15: Jay 3C 34
Shackleton Cl. CO4: Colc 4H 15
Shaftesbury Av. CO12: Har 3G 27
Shakespeare Rd. CO3: Colc 5F 13
Shalfleet Ct. CO15: Clac S 3J 31
Shamrock Ho. CO15: Clac S 4G 35
Shanklin Cl. CO15: Clac S 3K 31
Shaw Cl. CO13: Kir C 3D 28
Shawlands Av. CO10: Gt Cor 4H 37
Shawlands Retail Pk. CO10: Sud 3H 37
Shears Cl. CO5: W Mer 6D 40
Shears Cres. CO5: W Mer 6D 40
Shearwater Ho. CO12: Har 3H 27
Sheepen Pl. CO3: Colc 3A 42 (3A 14)
Sheepen Rd. CO3: Colc 3K 13
Sheepshead Hill CO10: Gt Cor 5J 37

Sheering Wlk. CO2: Colc 2B 22
Sheerwater M. CO4: A'lgh, Colc 3J 15
Shelley Av. CO5: Tip 5J 39
  CO10: Gt Cor 5H 37
Shelley La. CO16: L Cla 2J 31
Shelley Rd. CO3: Colc 5F 13
  CO16: Clac S 6D 30
Shepherd Dr. CO4: Colc 7A 6
Shepherd's Cft. CO3: S'way 6D 12
Sheppard Cl. CO16: Clac S 5G 31
Sherborne Cl. CO13: Kir C 3D 28
Sherbourne Rd. CO4: Colc 4H 15
Sheridan Wlk. CO3: Colc 5F 13
Sheriffs Way CO15: Clac S 4H 31
Sherwood Cl. CO4: Colc 4F 15
  CO15: Clac S 5F 35
Sherwood Dr. CO15: Clac S 4F 35
Shewell Wlk. CO1: Colc 5B 42 (4B 14)
Shillito Cl. CO3: Colc 7F 13
Ship Ho. CO2: Colc 6F 15
Shipwrights, The CO7: W'hoe 4K 23
Shipyard Est. CO7: B'sea 7H 41
Shire La. CO6: W Ber 6F 5
Shirley Cl. CO15: Jay 3D 34
Shoreham Rd. CO15: Clac S 4F 35
Short Cut Rd. CO1: Colc 4A 42 (4A 14)
Short Lo. CO10: Gt Hol 7A 28
Short Wyre St. CO1: Colc 5C 42 (4B 14)
Shotley Cl. CO16: Clac S 1D 34
SHRUB END 1G 21
Shrub End Rd. CO2: Colc 2F 21
  CO3: Colc 2F 21
Shrubland Cl. CO15: Clac S 6A 32
Shrubland Rd. CO2: Colc 7D 42 (5C 14)
  CO11: Mist 4H 11
Siam Pl. CO10: Colc 4E 36
Siena M. CO2: Colc 7D 14
Silcock Cl. CO4: Colc 1E 14
Silcott St. CO7: B'sea 6G 41
Sillett Cl. CO16: Clac S 5G 31
Silvanus Cl. CO3: Colc 5K 13
Silver Birch Cl. CO2: Colc 2K 21
Silver Dawn Touring Pk. CO16: Clac S 7C 30
Silverthorn Cl. CO5: Tip 5K 39
Silverthorne Cl. CO2: Colc 1C 22
Simons La. CO1: Colc 6E 42 (5C 14)
Sinclair Cl. CO4: Colc 1B 14
Singer Av. CO15: Jay 5B 34
Singleton Ct. CO10: Gt Cor 6G 37
Sinnington End CO4: Colc 6E 6
Sioux Cl. CO4: Colc 6E 6
Siric Ho. CO2: Colc 7A 14
Sir Isaac's Wlk. CO1: Colc 5A 42 (4A 14)
Siskin Cl. CO4: Colc 3H 15
Sittang Cl. CO2: Colc 3J 21
Sitwell Cl. CO11: Law 3D 10
Skelmersdale Rd. CO15: Clac S 1J 35
Skelton Cl. CO4: Colc 3E 10
Skiphatch La. CO11: Hor X, L Bro 7H 11
Skyrmans Fee CO13: Kir C 4C 28
3ladbury's La. CO15: Clac S 1B 32
Slade Rd. CO15: Hol S 5B 32
Slate CO9: Hals 4C 38
Slaters Cl. CO13: Kir C 4D 28
Sloe Hill CO9: Hals 3A 38
Slough Farm Rd. CO9: Hals 3A 38
Slough La. CO7: A'lgh 7B 8
  CO7: Elm M 5K 15
Smallwood Rd. CO2: Colc 1H 21
Smeaton Cl. CO4: Colc 4E 6
Smeetham Hall La. CO10: Bulm 4A 36
Smiths Fld. CO1: Colc 6E 14
Smythe Cl. CO16: Clac S 1K 35
Smythies Av. CO1: Colc 5E 42 (4C 14)
Snape Cl. CO16: Clac S 7D 30
Snape Way CO13: Kir C 3D 28
Snowberry Gro. CO2: Colc 1C 22
Solway Cl. CO3: Colc 3G 15
Somerset Cl. CO2: Colc 1H 21
Somerset Way CO15: Jay 3C 34
Somers Rd. CO3: Colc 7G 13
Sonnell Cl. CO7: W'hoe 2K 23
Sorrel Cl. CO4: Colc 1J 13
Southcliff Cl. CO15: Clac S 7A 32
Southcliff Pde. CO14: Walt 3G 29
Southcliff Pk. CO15: Clac S 7K 31
Southcliff Prom. CO13: Frin S 5F 29
  CO14: Walt 4G 29
South Cl. CO9: Hals 5B 38
Southcroft Cl. CO13: Kir C 4A 28
Southgate Cres. CO5: Tip 5J 39
Southgreen Gdns. CO16: Clac S 7F 31
Southland Cl. CO4: Colc 2E 14
Southland Dr. CO4: Colc 2E 14
South Strand CO11: Law 2E 10
South St. CO2: Colc 7A 42 (5A 14)
  CO11: Mann 3F 11

Sth. Suffolk Bus. Cen.—Thanet Wlk.

Sth. Suffolk Bus. Cen. CO10: Sud 4G **37**
Southview Dr. CO14: Walt 3G **29**
CO15: Hol S 5E **32**
Southway CO2: Colc 6A **42** (5A **14**)
CO3: Colc 6A **42** (5A **14**)
CO7: B'sea 5H **41**
Southwold Way CO16: Clac S 6D **30**
Sovereign Cres. CO3: Colc 5J **13**
Spansey Cl. CO9: Hals 4A **38**
Sparling Cl. CO2: Colc 2J **21**
Sparlings, The CO13: Kir S 2A **28**
Sparrow Rd. CO10: Gt Cor 5H **37**
Sparrows Herne CO15: Clac S 5J **31**
Spartan Cl. CO6: Gt Hork 3H **5**
Speedwell Rd. CO2: Colc 2F **23**
Spencer Rd. CO2: Colc 3A **22**
Spendells Cl. CO14: Walt 7H **29**
Spenser Way CO15: Jay 3C **34**
Spicer Way CO10: Gt Cor 7H **37**
Spindle St. CO4: Colc 1H **13**
Spindle Wood CO4: Colc 6C **6**
Spindrift Way CO7: W'hoe 4J **23**
Spinnaker Cl. CO15: Clac S 4G **35**
Spinney, The CO6: W Ber 7E **4**
Spinneyfields CO5: Tip 4H **39**
Spire Chase CO10: Sud 1G **37**
Spirit Health Club .4A **12**
Spiritus Ho. CO2: Colc 6F **15**
Sportsway CO1: Colc 2C **42** (3B **14**)
Spratt's Marsh CO6: Gt Hork 1J **5**
Springbank Av. CO11: Law 4D **10**
Spring Chase CO7: B'sea 5G **41**
CO7: W'hoe 2K **23**
Spring Cl. CO4: Colc .7E **6**
CO16: Clac S 6F **31**
Springfield Rd. CO10: Sud 2E **36**
Springfields CO7: B'sea 6H **41**
Springfields Dr. CO2: Colc 1G **21**
Springham Dr. CO4: Colc 4C **6**
Springhill Cl. CO7: Gt Bro 2J **17**
Springlands Way CO10: Sud 1E **36**
Spring La. CO3: Colc .3G **13**
(not continuous)
CO3: Ford H 3A **12**
CO5: Fing 6K **23**
CO6: Eig G 3A **12**
CO6: W Ber 6E **4**
CO7: W'hoe 2K **23**
(not continuous)
SPRING LANE INTERCHANGE 3E **12**
SPRING LANE RDBT. 4G **13**
Spring Rd. CO5: Tip .6G **39**
CO7: B'sea 5H **41**
Spring Sedge Cl. CO3: S'way 4C **12**
Spring Valley La. CO7: A'lgh, Crock H 6K **7**
Spruce Av. CO4: Colc 3F **15**
Spruce Cl. CO5: W Mer 4B **40**
Spurgeon St. CO1: Colc 5E **14**
(not continuous)
Square, The CO2: Colc 1H **21**
CO5: W Mer 5B **40**
Squat La. CO12: Har .5F **27**
Squirrels Fld. CO4: Colc 5B **6**
Stable Cl. CO3: S'way 5E **12**
CO5: W Mer 4E **40**
Stablefield Rd. CO14: Walt 3E **28**
Stable M. CO5: W Mer 3E **40**
Stable Rd. CO2: Colc 7A **42** (6A **14**)
Stafford Cl. CO13: Kir C 4C **28**
Stalin Rd. CO2: Colc .7C **14**
Stallards Cres. CO13: Kir C 4C **28**
Stambridge Rd. CO15: Clac S 7F **31**
Stammers Rd. CO4: Colc 6B **6**
Standard Av. CO15: Jay 5A **34**
Standard Rd. CO1: Colc 5E **14**
Standley Rd. CO14: Walt 1H **29**
Stane Fld. CO6: M Tey 3C **18**
Stanfield Cl. CO3: S'way 1E **20**
Stanford Rd. CO4: Colc 1B **14**
Stanley Av. CO7: B'sea 5J **41**
Stanley Rd. CO7: W'hoe 3A **24**
CO9: Hals 3A **38**
CO10: Sud 3E **36**
CO15: Clac S 2E **34**
Stanley Wood Av. CO10: Sud 2F **37**
Stanley Wooster Way CO4: Colc 4G **15**
Stanmore Cl. CO16: Clac S 6G **31**
Stannard Way CO10: Gt Cor 5G **37**
Stanstead Pl. *CO9: Hals* *5C 38*
(off Stanstead Rd.)
Stanstead Rd. CO9: Hals 5C **38**
Stansted Rd. CO2: Colc 3C **22**
Stansted Way CO13: Frin S 4E **28**
STANWAY 1K **19**
STANWAY GREEN 7C **12**
Stanway Retail Pk. CO3: S'way 7D **12**
Stanway Western By-Pass CO3: S'way 6B **12**
Stanwell St. CO2: Colc 6B **42** (5B **14**)
Stanwyn Av. CO15: Clac S 1H **35**
Station App. CO12: Har 2K **27**
CO13: Frin S 5D **28**
Station La. CO12: Har 3H **27**
Station Rd. CO5: Tip .6G **39**
CO6: M Tey 2E **18**
CO7: A'lgh 3C **8**
CO7: Alr 4F **25**
CO7: B'sea 6G **41**
CO7: Frat 4K **25**
CO7: Thorr 7K **25**
CO7: W'hoe 4K **23**
CO10: Sud 4E **36**
CO11: Law 2D **10**
CO12: Har 2E **26**
(Coller Rd.)
CO12: Har 2J **27**
(Ferndale Rd.)
CO12: Har 3J **27**
(Kingsway)
CO15: Clac S 2J **35**
Station St. CO14: Walt 2G **29**
Station Yd. CO15: Clac S 1J **35**
Steam Mill Rd. CO11: Brad, Mist 7J **11**
Steed Cres. CO2: Colc 6C **14**
Steele Cl. CO6: M Tey 3D **18**
Stephen Cranfield Cl. CO5: Rhdge 5J **23**
Stephenson Ho. CO2: Colc 6A **14**
Stephenson Rd. CO4: Colc 4F **7**
CO15: Clac S 3A **32**
Stephenson Rd. W. CO15: Clac S 2K **31**
Sterling Cl. CO3: Colc 6E **12**
Stevens Cl. CO4: Colc 7A **6**
Stevenson App. CO10: Gt Cor 6H **37**
Stevens Wlk. CO4: Colc 4H **15**
Stewards Cl. CO13: Frin S 3D **28**
Stirrup M. CO3: S'way 5D **12**
Stockwell CO1: Colc 4B **42** (4B **14**)
Stoke Ash Cl. CO16: Clac S 1D **34**
Stokes, The CO14: Walt 1F **29**
Stonecrop CO4: Colc 1J **13**
Stonehall Dr. CO16: L Cla 2G **31**
Stonehill Way CO5: W Mer 5A **40**
Stoneleigh Pk. CO3: Colc, S'way 1F **21**
Stone Rd. CO7: Gt Bro 3K **17**
Stoney La. CO7: B'sea 4J **41**
Stonham Av. CO16: Clac S 7D **30**
Stopes Ho. CO1: Colc 4E **42**
Stores La. CO5: Tip .4G **39**
Stour Cl. CO12: Har, R'sy 5C **26**
Stourdale Cl. CO11: Law 4C **10**
Stour Gdns. CO10: Gt Cor 7H **37**
Stour Rd. CO12: Har .2J **27**
(not continuous)
Stour Sailing Club *3F 11*
(off Quay St.)
Stour St. CO10: Sud .4D **36**
CO11: Mann 3F **11**
Stour Vw. Av. CO11: Mist 3J **11**
Stourview Cl. CO11: Mist 3K **11**
Stour Vw. Ct. CO12: Har 2J **27**
Stour Wlk. CO4: Colc 1G **15**
Stow Ct. CO4: Colc 5B **6**
Straight Rd. CO3: Colc 5E **12**
CO4: Boxt 2A **6**
CO11: Brad 6K **11**
Stratford Pl. CO14: Walt 2G **29**
Stratford Rd. CO15: Hol S 5C **32**
Strawberry La. CO5: Tip 7J **39**
Straw La. CO10: Sud .4E **36**
Street, The CO7: A'lgh 2C **8**
CO10: Midd 7E **36**
CO13: Kir S 1A **28**
CO16: L Cla 1G **31**
Strikes Sudbury 2G **37**
Strood, The CO5: Pel, W Mer 1C **40**
Strood Cl. CO5: W Mer 4B **40**
Stuart Ho. CO1: Colc 3B **42** (3B **14**)
Stuart Pawsey Ct. CO7: W'hoe 3A **24**
Stuarts Dr. CO10: Sud 4G **37**
Stubbs Cl. CO11: Law 3D **10**
CO13: Kir C 4C **28**
Studd's La. CO4: Colc .6K **5**
Sturmer Ct. *CO2: Colc* *3C 22*
(off Queen Elizabeth Way)
Sudbourne Av. CO16: Clac S 7D **30**
SUDBURY 4F **37**
Sudbury Bus Station 4F **37**
Sudbury Rd. CO9: Hals 2C **38**
CO10: Bulm 5A **36**
Sudbury Sports Cen. 2F **37**
Sudbury Station (Rail) 4F **37**
Suffolk Av. CO5: W Mer 4D **40**
Suffolk Cl. CO4: Colc 2D **14**
CO15: Hol S 4D **32**
Suffolk Rd. CO10: Sud 3E **36**
Suffolk Sq. CO10: Sud 3E **36**
Suffolk St. CO14: Walt 2G **29**
Sullivan Cl. CO4: Colc 5G **15**
Sunbeam Av. CO15: Jay 6B **34**
Sunbeam Cl. CO5: Rhdge 4J **23**
Sundale Cl. CO15: Hol S 5E **32**
Sunningdale Way CO13: Kir C 3C **28**
Sunny Point CO14: Walt 6J **29**
Sunnyside Way CO16: L Cla 2F **31**
Surrey La. CO5: Tip .6G **39**
Sussex Gdns. CO15: Hol S 5D **32**
Sussex Rd. CO3: Colc 4J **13**
Sutton Pk. Av. CO3: Colc 1G **21**
Swallow Cl. CO2: Lay H 7G **21**
CO12: Har 6D **26**
Swallowdale CO2: Colc 1E **22**
CO15: Clac S 4J **31**
Swallow Wlk. CO9: Hals 4C **38**
Swan Cl. CO4: Colc .5G **15**
Swan Ct. *CO11: Mist* *4J 11*
(off Harwich Rd.)
Swandale CO15: Clac S 4J **31**
Swanfield Cotts. CO3: S'way 1J **19**
Swan Pas. CO1: Colc 4C **42** (4B **14**)
Sweden Cl. CO12: Har 3E **26**
Sweet Briar Rd. CO3: S'way 4C **12**
Swift Av. CO3: S'way 7C **12**
CO15: Jay 6C **34**
Sycamore Rd. CO4: Colc 3F **15**
CO10: Gt Cor 4H **37**
Sycamore Way CO13: Kir C 4B **28**
CO15: Clac S 1F **35**
Sydney St. CO2: Colc 3D **22**
CO7: B'sea 7H **41**
Symonds Ct. CO9: Hals 3C **38**
Syringa Ct. *CO4: Colc* *4G 15*
(off Blackthorn Av.)

T

Tabor Cl. CO7: B'sea 4H **41**
Tabor Rd. CO1: Colc .4E **14**
Talavera Cres. CO2: Colc 2J **21**
Talbot Av. CO15: Jay 6C **34**
Talbot Rd. CO10: Sud 1F **37**
Talbot St. CO12: Har .2J **27**
Talcott Rd. CO2: Colc 2C **22**
Talisman Cl. CO5: Tip 4H **39**
Talisman Wlk. CO5: Tip 4H **39**
Tall Trees CO4: Colc .7A **6**
Tally Ho CO4: Colc 6D **6**
Tamarisk Way CO4: Colc 3G **15**
CO15: Jay 6C **34**
Tamworth Chase CO2: Colc 2C **22**
Tangerine Cl. CO4: Colc 5F **15**
Tan La. CO16: L Cla 1J **31**
Tanner Cl. CO16: Clac S 1E **34**
Tapsworth Cl. CO16: Clac S 6F **31**
Tapwoods CO3: Colc .4G **13**
Tara Cl. CO4: Colc 2F **15**
Tarragona M. CO2: Colc 7D **14**
Tarragon Cl. CO5: Tip 5G **39**
Tarrett Dr. CO1: Colc 5E **14**
Tawell M. CO5: Tip 5H **39**
Taylor Ct. CO1: Colc 4B **42** (4B **14**)
Taylor Dr. CO11: Law 3E **10**
Taylor's Rd. CO5: Rhdge 4H **23**
Tayspill Ct. *CO2: Colc* *1H 21*
(off Coats Hutton Rd.)
Teal Cl. CO4: Colc 3J **15**
Tedder Cl. CO2: Colc 7C **14**
Telford Rd. CO15: Clac S 3A **32**
Telford Way CO4: Colc 4F **7**
Temple Cl. CO13: Frin S 4E **28**
Temple Ct. CO4: Colc 1F **15**
Temple Rd. CO2: Colc 2G **21**
Templewood Rd. CO4: Colc 2G **15**
Tenpenny Hill CO7: Alr, Thorr 6H **25**
Tenpin
Colchester **1C 42** (**2B 14**)
Terling Cl. CO2: Colc 3C **22**
Terndale CO15: Clac S 5J **31**
Tern M. CO7: W'hoe .4K **23**
Terrace Hall Chase
CO6: Gt Hork 4J **5**
Tew Cl. CO5: Tip 5H **39**
Tewkesbury Rd. CO15: Clac S 7H **31**
Tey Gdns. CO6: L Tey 3A **18**
Thanet Wlk. *CO5: Rhdge* *4J 23*
(off High St.)

A-Z Colchester 61

Thatchers Dr. CO7: Elm M 5D 16
Thaxted Wlk. CO2: Colc 4C 22
The . . . .
  Names prefixed with 'The' for example 'The
  Acorns' are indexed under the main name such
  as 'Acorns, The'
Thelsford Wlk. CO4: Colc 4H 15
Third Av. CO9: Hals 4E 38
  CO12: Har 4H 27
  CO13: Frin S 6C 28
  CO14: Walt 6J 29
  CO15: Clac S 7B 32
Thirtle Cl. CO16: Clac S 5G 31
Thistledown CO4: Colc 7D 6
Thomas Benold Wlk. CO2: Colc 4B 22
Thomas Ct. CO1: Colc 4D 14
Thomas Rd. CO15: Clac S 7G 31
Thomas St. CO7: B'sea 6H 41
Thomas Wakley Cl. CO4: Colc 5B 6
Thompson Av. CO3: Colc 5F 13
Thornbury Rd. CO15: Clac S 7J 31
Thorndon Cl. CO16: Clac S 7D 30
Thornhill Cl. CO13: Kir C 3D 28
Thorns Way CO14: Walt 2E 28
Thornton Dr. CO4: Colc 1B 14
Thornwood CO4: Colc 6B 6
Thornwood CO5: W Mer 6D 40
Thoroughgood Rd. CO15: Clac S 1J 35
Thorpe Rd. CO15: Clac S 5J 31
  CO16: Clac S, L Cla 2K 31
Thorpe Wlk. CO4: Colc 4H 15
Thorrington Tide Mill 1G 41
Thracian Cl. CO2: Colc 2G 21
Three Crowns Rd. CO4: Colc 1A 14
Three Gates Cl. CO9: Hals 5A 38
Threshers End CO3: S'way 6D 12
Thrushdale CO15: Clac S 5J 31
Thurlston Cl. CO4: Colc 2F 15
Thyme Rd. CO5: Tip 5G 39
Tiberius Cl. CO4: Colc 5D 6
Tidings Hill CO9: Hals 6B 38
Tiffin Dr. CO5: Tip 5J 39
Tile Barn La. CO11: Law 1G 9
Tile Ho. La. CO6: Gt Hork 2H 5
Timber Hill CO1: Colc 5E 14
Tippett Cl. CO4: Colc 5G 15
TIPTREE 5H 39
Tiptree Golf Driving Range 5K 39
Tiptree Hall La. CO5: Tip 7F 39
TIPTREE HEATH .7F 39
Tiptree Heath Nature Reserve 7F 39
Tiptree Vis. Cen. & Mus. 6J 39
Titania Cl. CO4: Colc 4H 15
Titus Way CO4: Colc 4D 6
Toga Cl. CO2: Colc 2G 21
Tokely Rd. CO7: Frat 1K 25
TOLLESHUNT KNIGHTS 7K 39
Tollgate Bus. Pk. CO3: S'way 6B 12
Tollgate Cen., The CO3: S'way 6C 12
Tollgate Ct. CO3: S'way 5C 12
Tollgate Dr. CO3: S'way 5B 12
Tollgate E. CO3: S'way 5C 12
Tollgate Rd. CO3: S'way 5C 12
TOLLGATE RDBT. .5B 12
Tollgate W. CO3: S'way 6B 12
Tolliday Cl. CO7: W'hoe 2J 23
Tony Webb Cl. CO4: Colc 6E 6
Topnotch Health Club
  Highwoods 5E 6
Topsfield CO10: Gt Cor 7H 37
Torch Wlk. CO4: Colc 4C 6
Tortosa Cl. CO2: Colc 7D 14
Totlands Dr. CO15: Clac S 4J 31
Totteridge Cl. CO16: Clac S 6G 31
Toucan Way CO15: Clac S 5J 31
Tourist Info. Cen.
  Clacton-on-Sea 1J 35
  Colchester 4C 42 (4B 14)
  Sudbury .4E 36
  Walton-on-the-Naze 2H 29
Tower Cvn. Pk. CO15: Jay 6A 34
Tower Cut CO7: B'sea 6H 41
Tower Rd. CO7: W'hoe 2K 23
  CO15: Clac S 3H 35
Towers, The CO15: Clac S 1K 35
Tower St. CO7: B'sea 7H 41
Townsend Rd. CO5: Tip 3G 39
Towse Cl. CO4: Colc 6F 31
Trafalgar Ct. CO7: B'sea 4H 41
Trafalgar Rd. CO3: Colc 5E 12
  CO10: Sud 2G 37
  CO15: Clac S 3H 35
Trajan Cl. CO4: Colc 4D 6
Tranter Dr. CO4: Colc 6A 6
Travers Rd. CO2: Colc 3B 22

Treadwheel Ho. CO12: Har 3F 27
Tree Cl. CO15: Clac S 4J 31
Treetops CO4: Colc 7D 6
Treetops Ct. CO4: Colc 5B 6
Trevor Bailey Dr. CO1: Colc 2C 42 (3B 14)
Triangle Shop. Cen. CO13: Frin S 3D 28
Trimley Cl. CO16: Clac S 7E 30
Trinity Cl. CO5: W Mer 4C 40
  CO7: W'hoe 3A 24
  CO11: Mann 4F 11
Trinity Ct. CO9: Hals 4B 38
Trinity Ho. CO12: Har 3F 27
  (off Williamsburg Av.)
Trinity M. CO5: W Mer 4C 40
Trinity Rd. CO9: Hals 4A 38
  CO11: Mann 4F 11
Trinity Sq. CO1: Colc 5B 42 (4B 14)
Trinity St. CO1: Colc 5B 42 (4B 14)
  CO9: Hals 4A 38
Trippier Ho. CO4: Colc 4G 15
  (off Blackthorn Av.)
Triumph Av. CO15: Jay 5B 34
Triumph Cl. CO4: Colc 6G 15
Trowel Pl. CO2: Colc 3A 22
Truman Bldg., The CO6: W Ber 6F 5
Trunette Rd. CO15: Clac S 1F 35
Tryon Cl. CO9: Hals 4A 38
Tubswick M. CO4: Colc 6A 6
Tudor Cl. CO7: B'sea 4G 41
  CO10: Sud 2E 36
  CO14: Walt 7H 29
  CO15: Jay 3D 34
Tudor Ct. CO5: W Mer 4C 40
  CO10: Sud 1E 36
  CO15: Jay 4C 34
Tudor Grn. CO10: Sud 1E 36
Tudor Pde. CO15: Jay 3D 34
Tudor Rd. CO10: Sud 1E 36
Tudor Rose Cl. CO3: S'way 4C 12
Tudwick Rd. CO5: Tip 7J 39
Tufnell Way CO4: Colc 1J 13
Tulip Wlk. CO4: Colc 4F 15
Tulip Way CO16: Clac S 7F 31
Tumulus Way CO2: Colc 2F 21
Turbine Rd. CO4: Colc 1J 13
Turkentine Cl. CO10: Gt Cor 6K 37
Turkey Cock La. CO3: S'way 1J 19
  CO6: Eig G 3A 12
Turner Av. CO11: Law 2D 10
Turner Cl. CO7: W'hoe 3A 24
  CO10: Sud 1G 37
  CO16: Clac S 5G 31
Turner Ri. Retail Pk. CO4: Colc 2B 14
Turner Rd. CO4: Colc 6B 6
Turnip Lodge La. CO7: Elm M 4A 16
Turnpike Cl. CO4: L'ham 3G 7
  CO7: L'ham 3G 7
Turnstile Sq. CO2: Colc 7K 13
Turnstone End CO4: Colc 3H 15
Turpins Av. CO15: Clac S 6B 32
Turpins Cl. CO15: Clac S 6D 32
Turpins La. CO13: Kir C, Kir S 2B 28
Tusset M. CO4: Colc 4E 12
Tweed Cl. CO9: Hals 5A 38
Twining Rd. CO3: Colc 7E 12
Tydeman Cl. CO3: S'way 7C 12
Tyed Cft. CO3: S'way 5D 12
Tyehurst Cres. CO4: Colc 1E 14
Tye La. CO7: W'hoe 1C 24
Tye Rd. CO7: Elm M 4C 16
Tyler Av. CO16: Clac S 1E 34
Tyler St. CO12: Har 2E 26
Tylneys Rd. CO9: Hals 2D 38
Tyndale Dr. CO15: Jay 3D 34
Tynedale Ct. CO4: Colc 6D 6
Tynedale Sq. CO4: Colc 6D 6
Tythings, The CO9: Hals 5A 38

U

Una Rd. CO12: Har 3D 26
Union Rd. CO15: Jay 4D 34
United Way CO4: Colc 4A 6
Unity Cl. CO2: Colc 7D 14
University of Essex
  Colchester Campus 7H 15
  Sports Cen. 7J 15
Upland Cres. CO5: W Mer 4C 40
Upland Dr. CO4: Colc 1E 14
Upland Rd. CO5: W Mer 4C 40
Uplands Cl. CO15: Clac S 3G 35
Uplands Cres. CO10: Sud 2E 36
Uplands Rd. CO10: Sud 2E 36
  CO15: Clac S 3G 35

Up. Branston Rd. CO15: Clac S 7G 31
Up. Chapel St. CO9: Hals 3B 38
UPPER DOVERCOURT 5D 26
Up. East St. CO10: Sud 3F 37
Up. Fenn Rd. CO9: Hals 3D 38
Up. Fourth Av. CO13: Frin S 5D 28
Up. Haye La. CO5: Fing 7E 22
Up. Park Rd. CO7: B'sea 5G 41
  CO15: Clac S 1G 35
Upper Reeve CO10: Gt Cor 7H 37
Up. Second Av. CO13: Frin S 5C 28
Up. Third Av. CO13: Frin S 5C 28
Up. Trinity Rd. CO9: Hals 4B 38
Upper Tye CO10: Gt Cor 6J 37
Upton Cl. CO6: W Ber 6D 4

V

Vale Cl. CO4: Colc 1G 15
Valence Way CO15: Clac S 7J 31
Valens Cl. CO4: Colc 4C 6
Valenta Cl. CO4: Colc 5E 14
Valentines Dr. CO4: Colc 2E 14
Valentinus Cres. CO2: Colc 1B 22
Valfreda Way CO7: W'hoe 3K 23
Valleybridge Rd. CO15: Clac S 6K 31
Valley Cl. CO3: S'way 1E 20
Valley Cres. CO6: W Ber 7E 4
Valley Farm Holiday Pk. CO15: Clac S 5A 32
Valley Rd. CO4: Colc 7H 15
  CO7: W'hoe 4A 24
  CO12: Har 5C 26
  CO15: Clac S 6J 31
Valley Vw. CO6: W Ber 7E 4
Valley Vw. Cl. CO4: Colc 6C 6
Valley Wlk. CO14: Walt 3E 28
Vallis Way CO5: Tip 4J 39
  (off Grove Rd.)
Valonia Dr. CO7: W'hoe 4J 23
Van Dyck Rd. CO3: Colc 6G 13
Vanessa Dr. CO7: W'hoe 3K 23
Vansittart St. CO12: Har 2J 27
Vaux Av. CO12: Har 6E 26
Vauxhall Av. CO15: Jay 6B 34
Vega Cl. CO1: Colc 5E 14
Ventnor Dr. CO15: Clac S 3K 31
Ventura Dr. CO1: Colc 5E 14
Vermont Cl. CO15: Clac S 7K 31
Veronica Wlk. CO4: Colc 4G 15
Vicarage Ct. CO2: Colc 1F 21
  CO9: Hals 3A 38
Vicarage Fld. CO10: Gt Cor 6H 37
Vicarage Gdns. CO15: Clac S 2G 35
Vicarage La. CO14: Walt 2G 29
Vicarage Mdw. CO9: Hals 4B 38
Viceroy Cl. CO2: Colc 1D 22
Victoria Av. CO13: Kir S 2B 28
Victoria Chase CO1: Colc 2A 42 (3A 14)
Victoria Cl. CO7: W'hoe 2K 23
Victoria Ct. CO12: Har 4H 27
  CO15: Clac S 1H 35
Victoria Cres. CO11: Law 3E 10
Victoria Esplanade CO5: W Mer 6D 40
Victoria Gdns. CO4: Colc 7D 6
Victoria M. CO5: W Mer 5D 40
Victoria Pl. CO1: Colc 5D 14
  (Cannon St.)
  CO1: Colc 5C 42 (4B 14)
  (Long Wyre St.)
  CO7: B'sea 6H 41
Victoria Rd. CO3: Colc 6J 13
  CO14: Walt 2G 29
  CO15: Clac S 1K 35
Victoria St. CO12: Har 3J 27
Victor Rd. CO1: Colc 5D 14
Victory Cl. CO3: Colc 5E 12
  CO15: Clac S 3H 35
Victory Pl. CO5: W Mer 5A 40
Victory Rd. CO5: W Mer 5A 40
  CO15: Clac S 1G 35
Vienna Cl. CO12: Har 6F 27
Viking Way CO15: Hol S 5E 32
Village Cl. CO13: Kir C 3B 28
  CO16: L Cla 2G 31
Village Way CO13: Kir C 3B 28
Villa Rd. CO3: S'way 5C 12
Vince Cl. CO5: W Mer 5C 40
Vine Dr. CO7: W'hoe 1A 24
Vine Farm Rd. CO7: W'hoe 1A 24
Vine Pde. CO7: W'hoe 1A 24
Vine Rd. CO5: Tip 4G 39
Vinesse Rd. CO6: L Hork 1D 4
Vineway, The CO12: Har 3F 27
Vineyard Ga. CO2: Colc 6B 42 (5B 14)

Vineyard Steps CO2: Colc 5B **42** (4B **14**)
Vineyard St. CO2: Colc 6C **42** (4B **14**)
Vint Cres. CO3: Colc 5J **13**
Viola Wlk. CO4: Colc 4G **15**
Virginia Cl.
  CO15: Clac S, Jay 3D **34**
Viscount Dr. CO4: Colc 5E **6**
Vista Av. CO13: Kir S 1B **28**
Vista Rd. CO15: Clac S 7J **31**
Vitellus Cl. CO4: Colc 4D **6**
Vitoria M. CO2: Colc 2J **21**
  (off Salamanca Way)
Vivian Ct. CO14: Walt 2G **29**
Vortex Rd. CO4: Colc 1J **43**

W

Waddesdon Rd. CO12: Har 3J **27**
Wade Reach CO14: Walt 2E **28**
Wade Rd. CO15: Clac S 3A **32**
Wadley Cl. CO5: Tip 5J **39**
Wakefield Cl.
  CO1: Colc 3D **42** (3C **14**)
Waldegrave Cl. CO11: Law 4D **10**
Waldegrave Way CO11: Law 4D **10**
Walden Way CO13: Frin S 5D **28**
Waldingfield Rd. CO10: Sud 3F **37**
Walk, The CO6: Eig G 3A **12**
Wallace Rd. CO4: Colc 1A **14**
Wallis Ct. CO3: Colc 1E **20**
Wall M. CO2: Colc 3A **22**
Walls, The CO11: Mann 3F **11**
Walmer Cl. CO7: B'sea 5H **41**
Walnut Dr. CO4: Colc 5K **5**
Walnut Tree Ho. CO3: Colc 7H **13**
Walnut Tree La. CO10: Sud 4D **36**
Walnut Tree Way CO2: Colc 1H **21**
  CO5: Tip 3G **39**
Walnut Way CO7: B'sea 5G **41**
  CO15: Clac S 1F **35**
Walsingham Cl. CO10: Gt Cor 6J **37**
Walsingham Rd. CO2: Colc 6B **42** (5B **14**)
Walter Radcliffe Rd. CO7: W'hoe 5A **24**
Walter Radcliffe Way CO7: W'hoe 5A **24**
Walters Yd. CO1: Colc 4B **42** (4B **14**)
Waltham Way CO13: Frin S 5E **28**
Walton Maritime Mus. 1H **29**
WALTON-ON-THE-NAZE 2G **29**
Walton-on-the-Naze Station, The (Rail) . .3G **29**
Walton Pier Ten Pin Bowling Cen. 2H **29**
Walton Rd. CO13: Frin S 5D **28**
  CO13: Kir S .2A **28**
  (not continuous)
  CO14: Walt .5D **28**
  CO15: Clac S 1J **35**
Warde Chase CO14: Walt 2F **29**
Wargrave Rd. CO15: Clac S 7G **31**
Warham Rd. CO12: Har 5D **26**
Warley Way CO13: Frin S 4F **29**
Warner Way CO10: Sud 3G **37**
Warnham Cl. CO16: Clac S 5E **30**
Warren La. CO3: S'way 3B **20**
Warren Lingley Way CO5: Tip 4J **39**
Warren Rd. CO9: Hals 4A **38**
Warrens CO9: Hals 4A **38**
Warrens, The CO13: Kir C 4C **28**
Warwick Bailey Cl. CO4: Colc 1K **13**
Warwick Ct. CO2: Colc 7E **14**
  CO15: Clac S 1H **35**
Warwick Cres. CO15: Clac S 7H **31**
Warwick Rd. CO15: Clac S 1G **35**
Washford Gdns. CO15: Clac S 2G **35**
Washington Ct. CO3: Colc 6E **12**
Washington Rd. CO12: Har 5E **26**
Wash La. CO15: Clac S 3G **35**
  (not continuous)
Water Ct. CO15: Clac S 7H **31**
  (off Charles Burcart Gdns.)
Waterglade Retail Pk. CO15: Clac S 2H **35**
Waterhouse La. CO7: A'lgh 5E **8**
Water La. CO3: Colc 3K **13**
Waterside CO7: B'sea 7H **41**
Waterside La. CO2: Colc 7F **15**
Waterside Marina CO7: B'sea 7G **41**
Waterville M. CO2: Colc 1D **22**
Waterworks Dr. CO16: Clac S 6E **30**
Watsham Pl. CO7: W'hoe 1A **24**
Watson Rd. CO15: Clac S 1H **35**
Watts Rd. CO2: Colc 2H **21**
Wat Tyler Wlk. CO1: Colc 4B **42**
Wavell Av. CO2: Colc 7J **13**
Wavring Av. CO13: Kir C 3C **28**
Weavers Cl. CO3: Colc 6F **13**
Weaver's Ct. CO10: Sud 4E **36**

Weavers Ct. CO9: Hals 4B **38**
  CO12: Har .2J **27**
  (off Stour Rd.)
Weaver's La. CO10: Sud 4E **36**
Weavers Row CO9: Hals 4C **38**
Weavers Ter. CO10: Sud 4E **36**
  (off Weavers La.)
Wedgewood Dr. CO4: Colc 1A **14**
Weekes Cl. CO16: Clac S 6D **30**
Weetmans Dr. CO4: Colc 5C **6**
Weggs Willow CO4: Colc 4E **14**
Weir La. CO2: Colc 5D **22**
  CO5: Rhdge .5D **22**
Welham Cl. CO15: Clac S 4G **31**
Wellesley Rd. CO3: Colc 5A **14**
  CO15: Clac S 7H **31**
Well Fld. CO9: Hals 5C **38**
Wellfield Way CO13: Kir C 4B **28**
Wellhouse Av. CO5: W Mer 4E **40**
Wellington Rd. CO12: Har 1K **27**
Wellington St. CO2: Colc 6A **42** (5A **14**)
  CO7: B'sea .6H **41**
Well La. CO5: Ethpe 7E **18**
Wells Hall Rd. CO10: Gt Cor 6H **37**
Well Side CO6: M Tey 3C **18**
Wells Rd. CO1: Colc 3E **42** (3C **14**)
Well St. CO7: B'sea 5G **41**
WELSHWOOD PARK 1G **15**
Welshwood Pk. Rd. CO4: Colc 1G **15**
Wesley Av. CO4: Colc 3E **14**
West Av. CO15: Clac S 2H **35**
WEST BERGHOLT 6E **4**
Westbury Cl. CO6: Cop 1H **19**
West Cliff Theatre
  Clacton-on-Sea 2H **35**
Westcott Cl. CO16: Clac S 5G **31**
W. Dock Rd. CO12: Har 2D **26**
West End La. CO12: Har 6G **27**
West End Rd. CO5: Tip 7F **39**
Western App. CO3: S'way 5B **12**
Western Prom. CO7: B'sea 7F **41**
Western Rd. CO7: B'sea 6G **41**
Westhouse Wood Nature Reserve 7G **5**
Westlake Cres. CO7: W'hoe 2J **23**
Westlands Country Pk. 1F **21**
W. Lodge Rd. CO3: Colc 5K **13**
WEST MERSEA .5B **40**
West Mersea Yacht Club 5A **40**
Westminster Ct. CO2: Colc 7E **14**
  CO15: Clac S 7A **32**
  (off Connaught Gdns. E.)
Westmorland Cl. CO11: Mist 4J **11**
Weston Homes Community Stadium 4A **6**
Weston Rd. CO2: Colc 6D **14**
West Quay CO7: W'hoe 5K **23**
  (off The Quay)
Westridge Way CO15: Clac S 5K **31**
West Rd. CO9: Hals 4B **38**
  CO15: Clac S, Jay 4D **34**
Westside Cen. CO3: S'way 6A **12**
W. Stockwell St. CO1: Colc 4B **42** (4B **14**)
West St. CO2: Colc 6A **42** (5A **14**)
  CO5: Rhdge .4H **23**
  CO7: W'hoe .4K **23**
  CO12: Har .1J **27**
  CO14: Walt .2G **29**
West Vw. Cl. CO4: Colc 7D **6**
Westway CO1: Colc 1A **42** (2A **14**)
  CO3: Colc .3A **14**
Westwood Dr. CO5: W Mer 5E **40**
Westwood Hill CO4: Colc 7H **5**
West Yd. CO9: Hals 5B **38**
Wethersfield Rd. CO2: Colc 4C **22**
Wetzlar Ct. CO2: Colc 7D **14**
Weyland Dr. CO3: S'way 7D **12**
Weymouth Cl. CO15: Clac S 4G **35**
Whaley Rd. CO4: Colc 4E **14**
Wheatfield Rd. CO3: S'way 5D **12**
Wheatlands CO7: Elm M 5D **4**
Wheatsheaf Ct. CO1: Colc 7E **42** (5D **14**)
Wheeler Cl. CO4: Colc 5G **15**
Wheelers Cl. CO10: Sud 3G **37**
Wheelwright Pl. CO4: Colc 6A **6**
Wherry Cnr. CO11: Mann 3F **11**
  (off High St.)
Whinfield Av. CO12: Har 6E **26**
Whitebeam Cl. CO4: Colc 5K **5**
Whitefriars Way CO3: Colc 6G **13**
Whitegate Rd. CO7: B'sea 6J **41**
Whitehall Cl. CO7: Colc 7E **14**
Whitehall Ind. Est. CO2: Colc 7F **15**
White Hart La. CO6: W Ber 5D **4**
  CO12: Har .1J **27**
White Horse Av. CO9: Hals 5A **38**

White Ho. CO2: Colc 6A **14**
Whitehouse Farm Rd. CO5: Ethpe 7F **19**
Whitehouse La. CO6: W Ber 7D **4**
Whitethorn Cl. CO4: Colc 5F **15**
Whitewell Rd. CO2: Colc 6B **42** (5B **14**)
Whittaker Way CO5: W Mer 4B **40**
Wickham Rd. CO3: Colc 6K **13**
Wick La. CO7: A'lgh 2H **7**
  CO12: Har .6G **27**
  CO16: Wee H 1A **30**
Wick Rd. CO2: Colc 2F **23**
Wignall St. CO11: Law 4B **10**
Wilbye Cl. CO2: Colc 7H **13**
Wilkin Cl. CO3: Colc 7G **13**
Wilkin Dr. CO5: Tip 5H **39**
Willett Rd. CO2: Colc 1H **21**
William Bleakley M.
  CO12: Har .4E **26**
William Boys Cl. CO4: Colc 3F **15**
William Cl. CO7: W'hoe 7A **16**
William Dr. CO15: Clac S 2G **35**
William Groom Av. CO12: Har 5F **27**
William Harris Way CO2: Colc 3B **22**
Williamsburg Av. CO12: Har 3F **27**
Williamson Ho. CO1: Colc 6E **42**
William Sparrow Ct. CO7: W'hoe 2A **24**
Williams Wlk.
  CO1: Colc 4B **42** (4B **14**)
William Wood Ho. CO10: Sud 4E **36**
  (off School St.)
Willingham Way CO4: Colc 4G **15**
Willoughby Av. CO5: W Mer 5D **40**
Willow Av. CO13: Kir S 4B **28**
Willow Cvn. Pk. CO14: Walt 6H **29**
Willow Cl. CO7: A'lgh 4F **7**
  CO7: B'sea .6F **41**
  CO10: Sud .5E **36**
Willow Pk. CO6: Cop 1J **19**
Willows, The CO2: Colc 1C **22**
Willow Tree Ct. CO4: Colc 3G **15**
  (off Hawthorn Av.)
Willow Wlk. CO5: Tip 3G **39**
Willow Way CO9: Hals 4A **38**
  CO12: Har .5E **26**
  CO15: Jay 5D **34**
Wilmington Rd. CO4: Colc 1E **14**
Wilson Cl. CO7: W'hoe 2J **23**
Wilson Marriage Rd. CO4: Colc 2E **14**
Wilson's La. CO6: M Tey 3B **18**
Wimborne Gdns. CO13: Kir C 3D **28**
Wimpole Rd. CO1: Colc 5D **14**
Winchelsea Pl. CO7: B'sea 4H **41**
Winchester Rd. CO2: Colc 6C **14**
  CO13: Frin S 5E **28**
Windermere Ct. CO15: Clac S 1K **35**
  (off Marine Pde. E.)
Windermere Rd. CO10: Sud 3G **37**
  CO15: Hol S 5B **32**
Windham Rd. CO10: Sud 3G **37**
Windmill Cl. CO10: Gt Cor 7H **37**
Windmill Ct. CO4: Colc 6A **6**
  CO6: Cop 2H **19**
WINDMILL GREEN 4G **39**
Windmill Grn. Pl. CO5: Tip 4G **39**
Windmill Pk. CO15: Clac S 6J **31**
Windmill Rd. CO9: Hals 4A **38**
  CO11: Brad .5K **11**
Windmill Vw. CO5: Tip 4G **39**
Windsor Av. CO15: Clac S 1G **35**
Windsor Cl. CO2: Colc 2C **22**
Windsor Ct. CO1: Colc 5E **14**
  (off Hythe Hill)
  CO7: B'sea .5H **41**
Windsor Ho. CO5: W Mer 4D **40**
  (off Carrington Ct.)
Windsor Pl. CO10: Sud 4G **37**
Windsor Rd. CO5: W Mer 4D **40**
Windsor Rd. Folley
  CO5: W Mer 4D **40**
Winnock Rd. CO1: Colc 7D **42** (5C **14**)
  (not continuous)
Winnocks CO1: Colc 7D **42** (5C **14**)
Winsley Rd. CO1: Colc 7E **42** (5D **14**)
Winsley Sq. CO1: Colc 6D **14**
Winston Av. CO3: Colc 7H **13**
  CO5: Tip 5J **39**
Winston Way CO9: Hals 2D **38**
Winstree Cl. CO2: Colc 7F **21**
Winstree Rd. CO3: S'way 5D **12**
Winterbournes CO14: Walt 3E **28**
Winthrop Cl. CO10: Sud 2K **37**
Wistaria Pl. CO16: Clac S 6F **31**
Wisteria Cl. CO4: Colc 4G **15**
  (off Blackthorn Av.)
Witch Elm CO12: Har 5E **26**

Witting Cl. CO16: Clac S 6G 31
Witton Wood La. CO13: Frin S 5B 28
Wittonwood Rd. CO13: Frin S 5C 28
WIVENHOE 4K 23
Wivenhoe Cross CO7: W'hoe 2A 24
Wivenhoe Park 6H 15
Wivenhoe Pk. Cnr. CO7: Elm M 6J 15
Wivenhoe Rd. CO7: Alr 5C 24
  CO7: Crock H 2A 16
Wivenhoe Sailing Club 5A 24
Wivenhoe Station (Rail) 4K 23
Woburn Av. CO13: Kir C 3B 28
Woden Av. CO3: S'way 7D 12
Wolseley Av. CO15: Jay 6C 34
Wolton Rd. CO2: Colc 1H 21
Wood Barn La. CO11: A'lgh, Law 1H 9
Woodberry Way
  CO14: Frin S, Walt 3F 29
Woodbridge Gro. CO16: Clac S 7D 30
Woodcock Cl. CO4: Colc 5G 15
Woodfield Cl. CO14: Walt 3E 28
Woodfield Dr. CO5: W Mer 4B 40
Wood Fld. End CO2: Lay H 7G 21
Woodford Cl. CO15: Clac S 3J 31
Wordhill Bus. Pk. CO10: Sud 1F 37
Woodhull Cl. CO10: Sud 2E 36
Woodhall Rd. CO10: Sud 2E 36
Woodhouse La. CO6: Gt Hork 4G 5
Woodland Dr. CO3: Colc, S'way 6F 13
Woodlands CO1: Colc 7E 42
  CO4: Colc 2H 15
  CO16: Clac S 3D 34
Woodlands, The CO7: B'sea 5G 41

Woodlands Cl. CO15: Clac S 3K 31
Woodland Way CO7: W'hoe 3K 23
Wood La. CO15: Clac S 1B 32
Woodpecker Cl. CO4: Colc 3H 15
Woodpeckers CO10: Sud 5E 36
Woodrows La. CO16: Clac S 5E 30
Woodrow Way CO4: Colc 4G 15
Woodrush End CO3: S'way 5B 12
Woods Ct. CO4: Colc 1K 13
Woodside CO14: Walt 4F 29
Woodside Cl. CO4: Colc 2G 15
Woodstock CO5: W Mer 4C 40
Wood Vw. CO5: Tip 6J 39
Woodview Cl. CO4: Colc 6F 7
Woolner Rd. CO16: Clac S 5G 31
Woolwich Rd. CO16: Clac S 6F 31
Worcester Cres. CO7: Alr 4F 25
Worcester Rd. CO1: Colc 3D 42 (3C 14)
Wordsworth Rd. CO3: Colc 5F 13
Wordsworth Way CO16: Clac S 6D 30
Workhouse Rd. CO6: L Hork 1D 4
                     (not continuous)
Worsdell Way CO4: Colc 1B 14
Worthing M. CO15: Clac S 4F 35
Worthington Way CO3: Colc 7F 13
Wrabness Rd. CO12: R'sy 5A 26
Wren Cl. CO3: S'way 7C 12
Wrendale CO15: Clac S 5J 31
Wren Ho. CO3: Colc 6F 13
                     (off Christine Chase)
Writtle Cl. CO16: Clac S 7E 30
Wroxham Cl. CO3: Colc 5H 13

Wryneck Cl. CO4: Colc 7B 6
Wych Elm CO2: Colc 1C 22
Wycliffe Gro. CO1: Colc 1A 42 (2A 14)
Wyedale Dr. CO3: Colc 6E 12
Wyncolls Rd. CO4: Colc 4E 6
Wyndham Cl. CO2: Colc 4D 22
Wyndham Cres. CO15: Clac S 7K 31
Wyvern Ct. CO7: W'hoe 3K 23

Y

Yale M. CO4: Colc 6D 6
Yarmouth Cl. CO16: Clac S 5G 31
Yew Tree Cl. CO4: Colc 3G 15
Yew Way CO15: Jay 6C 34
Yorick Av. CO5: W Mer 5C 40
Yorick Rd. CO5: W Mer 5C 40
York Cl. CO10: Sud 2E 36
York Mans. CO15: Hol S 6D 32
York Pl. CO1: Colc 3E 42 (3C 14)
York Rd. CO7: B'sea 6G 41
  CO10: Sud 3E 36
  CO15: Hol S 5C 32
York St. CO11: Mann 3F 11
Yorktown Cl. CO12: Har 3G 27
Young Cl. CO16: Clac S 6F 31
Ypres Rd. CO2: Colc 7B 14

Z

Zinnia M. CO16: Clac S 7F 31

SAFETY CAMERA INFORMATION

PocketGPSWorld.com's CamerAlert is a self-contained speed and red light camera warning system for SatNavs and Android or Apple iOS smartphones/tablets. Visit www.cameralert.com to download.

Safety camera locations are publicised by the Safer Roads Partnership which operates them in order to encourage drivers to comply with speed limits at these sites. It is the driver's absolute responsibility to be aware of and to adhere to speed limits at all times.

By showing this safety camera information it is the intention of Geographers' A-Z Map Company Ltd. to encourage safe driving and greater awareness of speed limits and vehicle speed. Data accurate at time of printing.

Printed and bound in the United Kingdom by Gemini Press Ltd., Shoreham-by-Sea, West Sussex
Printed on materials from a sustainable source